Healing
Yourself

Books by Walter Weston:

Healing Yourself

A PRACTICAL GUIDE

WALTER WESTON

HAMPTON ROADS
PUBLISHING COMPANY, INC.

for the evolving human spirit

Cover art by Frank Riccio
Cover design by Mayapriya Long

For information write:

Hampton Roads Publishing Company, Inc.
134 Burgess Lane
Charlottesville, VA 22902

Or call: (804)296-2772
FAX: (804)296-5096
e-mail: hrpc@hrpub.com
Web site: http://www.hrpub.com

If you are unable to order this book from your local
bookseller, you may order directly from the publisher.
Quantity discounts for organizations are available.
Call 1-800-766-8009, toll-free.

Library of Congress Catalog Card Number
98-72218

ISBN 1-57174-091-0

10 9 8 7 6 5 4 3 2 1

Printed on acid-free paper in Canada

TABLE OF CONTENTS

Part Three: Healing Your Relationships

Part Four: Healing Your Body

Beginning

Welcome to *Healing Yourself* and a rewarding new journey.

Healing Yourself provides all the knowledge, processes, and skills needed for you to restore your own physical, emotional, spiritual, and interpersonal health.

It is based upon spiritual healing, the world's most widely used healing approach, which is rooted in the belief that God heals the sick through prayer and touch.

Our spiritual healing approach is based upon a scientific understanding of how healing works, plus the experience of those who practice healing throughout the world. More than a thousand clinical studies provide us with a model for understanding and practicing self-healing that you can trust. For the first time, we have a model that promises predictable and consistent healing outcomes.

Science and Experience

I found neither theology nor metaphysics to be particularly helpful in my understanding of how spiritual healing works. What you are about to read is based upon scientific studies and experience.

I do believe in God as the creator and sustainer of all life. I do believe that God wants everyone to be healthy. I do believe that healing prayer and touch bring the power of God into your life and into the life of the world.

Healing Yourself clarifies our understanding of prayer, showing that we are partners with God in prayer. Science indicates that when we pray, we personally emit a 7.83 hertz frequency of energy that is programmed to produce the optimum conditions for life. Believers call this energy God's power or healing flow.

Emotional Healing

You will learn to release all the emotional trauma and hurts of your life, along with any existing destructive emotional states. You will learn to replace these with God's love, peace, and joy. Complete emotional healing is now possible as never before.

The mind-body connection in disease is well established. Most disease is caused and sustained by emotional pain. Remove your emotional pain and your body tends to heal itself. Emotional Release Therapy may be all you need to begin reversing the course of your medical condition.

Physical Healing

You will learn to use your own healing touch for physical healing. Research studies confirm that healing touch initiates and accelerates physical healing, even regenerating tissue and organs. Only emotional pain interferes with this healing process.

Interpersonal Healing

You will learn to harmonize your human energy fields with those of loved ones, removing the rough edges of relationships and replacing them with ongoing peace and cooperation.

Spiritual Renewal

Throughout *Healing Yourself* you will be using prayer and other spiritual disciplines to fill yourself with God, through whom new life flows. When your hurts have been healed, you will experience God far more deeply than you ever have. Rejoice in these unexpected blessings and the new life God brings you.

The Case History of Jane

Jane's sudden healing demonstrates the crucial role that emotional pain plays in both disease and health.

Jane had accepted conventional medical treatment during her six-year fight with breast cancer, but finally her doctors told her there was nothing more they could do for her. She had lost the battle. Her primary care physician then referred her to me, a wellness counselor and spiritual healer.

The first question I asked was, "Jane, is there a hurt that haunts you every day of your life?"

She immediately began crying and answered, "Yes, my ex-husband."

Without seeking further information, I coached her into releasing the hurt from her heart into my hand.

Following forty minutes of this therapy, she reported her emotional heaviness was gone and she felt light. She left.

In the following week's session, Jane smiled in satisfaction as she stated, "I don't even think about my ex-husband anymore. I haven't felt this peaceful since I was a teenager."

At this session, she released other hurts from throughout her life. I then taught her how to practice Emotional Release Therapy upon herself.

Three weeks later she reported that an MRI showed that her cancer had shrunk by a third and her one tumor was closing in on itself. Six weeks later she was free of cancer.

For more than twenty years we have had clinical evidence that cancer feeds on emotional pain. Now we have a means for removing the emotional pain: Emotional Release Therapy. We have evidence that cancer cells normalize when there is no emotional pain to feed upon.

The Role of Conventional Medicine

If there is a tried and true conventional medical treatment, use it. For instance, if your physician suggests that your cancer be surgically removed, have it removed. Embark upon your own self-healing processes before each treatment and then continue them afterwards. Spiritual healing enhances the outcome of all medical treatment. It also protects you from most side effects of treatment.

Some conditions respond best to conventional care. If you have a diseased gall bladder, let the doctor remove it. Let the doctor remove your cataracts. Take antibiotics for infections. Have a cast placed upon your broken arm, then use healing touch to cut healing time in half. Use educated common sense.

Healing Yourself will be used by many persons whose medical condition responded poorly to conventional medical care. But it can also heal what you thought was damaged forever, such as damage to your heart muscle, liver, or spine. Many conditions respond poorly to conventional treatment because emotional pain hinders the body's ability to respond to treatment. Spiritual healing overcomes this limitation. Spiritual healing can also reprogram genetically encoded diseases.

Are the processes you learn in *Healing Yourself* guaranteed to cure your particular medical condition?

As will be shown, most diseases begin in the human energy fields, which then program the body to become ill. All diseases are reflected in the human energy fields. The exercises you will practice in *Healing Yourself* will restore the health of your human energy fields and empower them to cure your physical body. They do so in a consistent and predictable manner.

Your cure rests on my ability to convince you that you are competent enough to cure yourself. I know you are. It works for everyone who continues to follow the processes.

Your own self-healing has little if anything to do with your own perceived sense of personal worth, goodness, religious faith, or status. The only qualification for offering self-healing is your capacity to love yourself.

Love empowers God's healing flow. By combining love, prayer, and touch, we are bringing God's power into your life. Doing so restores health and wholeness, replacing the suffering of illness with God's creative purpose.

It is normal and O.K. to be skeptical. Your primary motivation must be your burning desire to fight for your health. Your hope comes from becoming convinced by the truth you are reading and by noting the positive results of the exercises.

We all tend to look for someone else to heal us; to find healing from outside ourselves. If you are reading this, you may have already concluded that you are your own best healer. So enjoy this rewarding new adventure in self-healing. May you be richly blessed as you seek to restore your own health and life.

PART ONE:

HEALING BASICS

1

Your Role

My role is to offer you the understanding, processes, and skills needed to help you regain optimum emotional and physical health.

Your role is to use *Healing Yourself* in the wisest possible ways. Here are some hints that will save you time and deepen your understanding of the processes through which you are being led.

Emotional Healing *Always* Comes First

Heal your emotions first. Whether you have an acute, chronic, or life-threatening condition, emotional healing *always* comes first.

Painful emotional states keep you unhappy, tired, and stressed out. They rob the health of your emotional energy field and hinder your best efforts at physical healing. Remove the painful emotional state and your body begins healing itself.

For twenty-seven years, I practiced primarily physical healing. I was aware of the dangerous role that emotions play in illness, but I knew of no consistent means for directly healing personal hurts.

Then, five years ago, I discovered a healing approach that quickly releases all emotional hurts and fixated destructive emotional states. As I observed the results of Emotional Release Therapy, I was amazed. By simply releasing emotional pain, I found that the symptoms of most diseases dramatically disappeared. As I coached patients on how to do so at home, it quickly became apparent that patients could just as effectively use this therapy upon themselves.

First, concentrate on releasing your emotional hurts. Do so even if you are not aware of any hurts. Everyone has hurts. Some are just better at hiding them from themselves.

Daily Commitment

Healing is not magic; it is a process. It took me two days to heal a bone-deep finger cut. I practiced healing daily for six weeks before my heart attack-damaged heart muscle was healed. That was before I knew about emotional healing.

Practice daily the healing steps in *Healing Yourself.* Learn to be comfortable and knowledgeable with each new healing skill. Make self-healing your number one daily priority. You are worth becoming healthy and whole. This is your motivation for making this your number one priority.

2

The Benefits Of Self-Healing

Few books have been written about self-healing. In fact, most literature on healing has led us to believe that self-healing is difficult if not impossible. Thirty years ago, I accepted those beliefs as true. But I was eventually in a position to observe enough successful self-healing efforts to conclude that self-healing was not only a beneficial option, but also a practical necessity.

As a busy pastor, I did not have the time to practice multiple sessions of spiritual healing with everyone who needed them. When a few of my shut-ins began requesting copies of the prayers for healing I had prayed with them, I began producing self-healing prayers for their use. I also provided directions on how to use their own touch for healing. I think I was more surprised by their positive outcomes than they were.

I went on to provide similar self-healing guidance to those with chronic and life-threatening diseases who seemed open to such an approach.

I observed successful self-healing efforts on conditions such as bed sores, skin diseases, trauma injuries, surgical wounds, arthritis, cancer, and heart disease.

After I began a second career as a writer and healer, I continued this approach. When I came upon the idea of Emotional Release Therapy, I soon discovered that it could be practiced as self-healing.

I have also practiced self-healing on myself to heal a bone-deep incision, a diseased heart, a chronically painful and swollen knee, colds, the flu, lung infections, skin infections, anger, fear, stress, and other ailments.

Barriers To the Practice of Self-Healing

From these experiences, I have learned to recognize these barriers to your successful practice of self-healing.

- **Resistance to the role of healer.** We have an image of a healer being separate and set apart from normal people, a superman for God, like the healers we have seen on television. That is an inaccurate image. Being a healer has nothing to do with your goodness, worthiness, religiousness, or power. But it *is* directly related to your capacity to love the ill. Who can be more concerned about your illness than you? The evidence is that when you are motivated by concern for yourself and intend to offer self-healing, you will generate the needed amount of healing flow through your own prayers and touch. Should you become discouraged, please come back and read this chapter.

- **Lack of self-confidence.** Self-confidence means, "I can do it." But in spiritual matters, most of us have poor self-images and, thus, little self-confidence. Healing is as easy to do as washing the dishes. When you become as comfortable practicing self-healing as you are washing dishes, you will produce miraculous self-healing outcomes. Just remember to take the time you need to feel comfortable and competent in the therapy you are practicing.

- **Being passive.** When we are ill, we tend to become passive, waiting for others to help us. We tend to lose our normal assertiveness. When my left knee had been swollen and painful for six weeks, I went to an orthopedic surgeon. He stated that I had so much bone loss that only a knee replacement would solve my problem. They say that necessity is the father of invention. Well, I returned home disappointed and finally remembered that I had been practicing spiritual healing for many years. Yes, up to that time, it had never occurred to me to try self-healing. I then did and it worked. You bought this book to do self-healing. Now, let your needs motivate you to get going and keep doing it.

You can do it.
You can do it.
You can do it.

3

Hope Versus Denial

When is it wise to have hope that you can overcome your medical condition?

When does your hope mask an unwillingness to face the medical reality of your condition?

In 1960, I took away a man's hope, hastening his death. At that time, I was the student-pastor of a rural church while attending graduate school. I met Don, twenty-six, a man suffering from late-stage cancer, on his farm. My heart immediately went out to him as Don proudly told me why he had lived two years beyond his death prognosis. He had sought reputed cures in San Diego, Mexico, Sweden, and New York. He was now attending a weekly healing service and he had plans to attend an upcoming faith-healing service in a distant city. Don was filled with hope and determined to try every possible alternative approach in order to become well.

One day his father-in-law visited me with his own special agenda. In seeking a cure, Don had squandered most of his financial assets, borrowing on his life insurance and putting a second mortgage on his farm. Don's wife and two sons would have few assets at his death. My heart went out to Don's family.

At that time, I knew next to nothing about this emerging new discipline, alternative medicine. If anything, I was cynical about it. And I certainly did not believe in faith healing at that time in my life. You can guess the rest of the story.

I discouraged Don. I brought him back to medical reality, just as my seminary had professionally taught me to do. I believed that Don was obviously in denial of reality. I stole his hope. And I watched in dismay as Don's health quickly deteriorated. When he died two weeks later, I wept in both grief and regret.

Fifteen Years Later — A Turnabout

In 1975, I had my own brush with death. I suffered a massive heart attack. The cardiologist's prognosis was that the muscle damage was so severe that I would not live out the year.

I came home from the hospital fearful, anxious, and depressed. By this time, I was knowledgeable about alternative medicine, but I was still a skeptic. I had accepted my cardiologist's prognosis, believing I would likely be dead within five months. Yet I possessed the hope that perhaps I might just be able to prolong my life a little beyond that.

I began with a week of educating myself about heart disease.

For two weeks, I battled nightly insomnia, until I worked through my fear of dying, using relaxation techniques, prayer, faith, and hope.

I took daily doses of 2,000 mg. of vitamin C and 800 IU of vitamin E.

I immediately began walking, progressing from severe angina pain after a hundred feet to an eventual two miles a day. (My cardiologist cautioned me that this was dangerous and no clinical evidence indicated any benefits. This was, of course, 1975.)

I maintained a low-cholesterol, low-fat diet and lost twenty pounds.

I lived each day as though it were my last, each morning genuinely rejoicing in the fact that I was alive.

For the first time in my life, I lived for myself. Daily, I chose activities that would bring me, and me alone, pleasure and satisfaction.

All this wellness wisdom grew out of my pastoral care training, for the Church had been a pioneer in holistic health.

My Own Exceptional Healing

By this time, I had been practicing spiritual healing for nearly a decade. But it never occurred to me that God could heal my damaged heart because I had never heard of it being done.

For emotional and spiritual support only, I practiced spiritual disciplines for an hour or two each morning. I read scriptures, used relaxation exercises, meditated, contemplated, visualized and prayed. (I will share guidance for these methods in later chapters.) Two weeks of these spiritual disciplines brought me the sacred peace that overcame my anxiety and fear of dying.

Physical healing. Then, in the sixth week of these spiritual disciplines, another miracle occurred. My dead heart muscle was healed, regenerated. Here is that experience:

21

Lying on my bed in the midst of a healing meditation, I found myself filled with a sense of God's presence. I felt a marvelous peace descend upon me, followed quickly by immense love, and then great joy! Tears of happiness streamed down my cheeks. I became aware of a Holy Presence. Brilliant white light filled my mind. I was in holy ecstasy. (The term *holy* is a traditional term for what the sensed presence of God feels like.)

Some unknown agent suddenly lifted my arms, which had been resting at my sides, and my hands were placed upon my chest. I was immersed in immense holiness, God. The hands resting upon my chest grew painfully hot. I felt the healing energy flowing throughout my whole body, down to even a tingling in my toes.

This peak experience of God seemed endless. Time stood still. A part of my intellect asked, "Am I being healed?" When I arose, I knew with inner certainty that my heart had been healed.

Medical confirmation. A few weeks later, during my three-month checkup, an EKG showed my heart muscle to be completely normal. The amazed cardiologist checked it against the ones originally taken in the coronary care unit and said, "This is impossible. Such a thing has never been reported in medical literature. You are a miracle patient!" He did not want to hear my story and refused to write it up for a medical journal, saying "No one would believe me."

Hope Is Usually an Appropriate Stance

My story probably mirrors your own journey. You have learned as much as possible about your medical condition. Although your medical prognosis may be bad, you have an abiding hope that you will get well. You are living a healthier life-style. You have likely used various forms of alternative medicine. You have turned to God for help.

You hope that by taking the steps provided in this book, you will be healed, restoring your own health and happiness.

You must always maintain your hope. Somehow, hope enhances whatever energies you possess and empowers your body's fight for survival. But are there times when your hope might be misguided?

Denial

Denial involves the emotional inability to either hear or accept the reality or dangers involved in a medical diagnosis. Denial might say, "It's not serious. I do not need any medical treatment. I'll just continue living as I always have."

Early denial can be beneficial. Denial allows the grim medical truth to sink in slowly as one becomes emotionally able to handle it, one bit at a time. But denial can also hold you in such a hypnotic-like state that you are unable to ever face the illness.

I think denial is best approached by talking to others about your fears and by embarking on a spiritual journey of faith. In doing so, you can begin to accept the seriousness of your medical condition and explore your treatment options.

Acceptance and Alternative Medicine

When our condition does not respond well to conventional treatment, it is crucial that we work through acceptance. To accept means to come to terms with the fact that we may have to live long-term with a chronic illness or possibly even die. Without this acceptance, when we eventually turn to alternative medicine, fear and panic may sabotage any approach we choose.

I have watched as panicky people quickly flitted from one alternative approach to another, giving no approach an opportunity to help them. They are suffering from magical thinking by wanting instant miracles. The same fear and panic can make patients suspicious of any alternative therapies they try. Neither conventional nor alternative medical approaches have much opportunity to be beneficial when faced with such negative attitudes.

Skeptical Loved Ones

Although it is becoming more acceptable to turn to alternative medicine, some of your loved ones may frown upon your use of spiritual healing. They may feel that you are in denial. If your situation warrants it, consider using this book quietly so they cannot discourage you.

4

Cheap Grace?

Must we struggle hard in order to get well?

Is there such a thing as a healing approach that is too easy to be acceptable?

A phone call inspired this chapter. Matt was canceling tomorrow's appointment for Emotional Release Therapy.

"Dr. Weston, I guess I owe you an explanation. I am in the midst of a twelve-step recovery program. It will probably take six more weeks of hard work to complete the step I am presently on. But, if I come to see you tomorrow night, all my emotional pain may be gone in one session. Isn't that cheap grace? Maybe I need to struggle through all my pain to learn any lessons they can teach me?"

I asked, "You mean no pain, no gain?"

"Yes, I think there is divine purpose in suffering and a spiritual blessing in having to claw my way out of emotional hell."

"If your wife had a choice between a vaginal delivery and a C-section, do you think she should choose a C-section because suffering more pain would make her a better mother?"

"No, of course not."

"If you studied ten hours for an exam and got a C, and if I studied two hours for the same exam and got an A, would God bless you more because you worked harder for your C?

"No, of course not."

"Do you come from a religious background in which undeserved suffering is often considered to be God's divine purpose for you?"

"Of course I do."

"I believe that suffering is evil, a part of the darkness that Christ came to help us overcome. I once prayed and touched a bone-deep cut in my finger for ten minutes, and God healed it in two days. In doing so, I avoided going to the Emergency Room. I was pleasantly surprised by the outcome and thanked God for his easy alternative. I did not think of this as cheap grace, but rather as the power of God's marvelous love."

"Can I still have some of that cheap grace of yours tomorrow night?"

I chuckled. "Of course you can, Matt."

Is Emotional Release Therapy too easy to be considered spiritual? Or, is it too wonderful to be true?

Is the scientific assurance about spiritual healing also too wonderful to be true?

My answer is the same as that of pioneering scientist Michael Faraday, who centuries ago in the midst of immense discoveries about the universe said, "Nothing is too wonderful to be true."

5

Scientific Foundations

Knowledge about spiritual healing comes from many sources. I found that popular beliefs about healing did not match my own personal experience. Some beliefs were clearly untrue. Some beliefs contradicted other beliefs. Only in scientific studies of prayer and healing did I find knowledge that matched my own experience and then took me beyond to greater insights that made me a better healer.

Thirty years ago, I, a healthy skeptic, unexpectedly became a healer. As a United Methodist minister, I was praying with a dying parishioner who became completely healed during our five-minute prayer together. After overcoming my initial shock, I became fascinated with healing, and then obsessed with learning everything I could about this mysterious new field of knowledge.

Eventually I turned to science and earned a Doctor of Ministry degree in healing research. Science provided me with an accurate and helpful new understanding of healing that I could find nowhere else.

Where but through science could I have watched videotape vividly display the enormous change in energy fields caused by healing touch?

Where but through science could I find objective evidence that a dozen theories I held about healing were not just speculation but actually true?

Where but through science could I find objective evidence that disease begins in the human energy fields months before it appears in the physical body?

I would not even trust the truth of my own observations without scientific evidence to back them up. Without scientific evidence to back up the approach I am teaching you, I would not have written this book. Here I share scientific knowledge that will help you practice effective self-healing.

A Theoretical Working Model

When scientists study religious phenomena such as healing, their approach requires changing vocabulary. God's healing power or flow are renamed subtle energy, life energy, or healing energy. Science is only capable of measuring *energies*. The human spiritual body is renamed *human energy fields*. It is the human energy fields that permit the existence of our souls, spirituality, and emotions. With vocabulary out of the way, we are now ready for the research.

All research begins with theories based upon observation, patterns, and intuition. The following theoretical working model is widely accepted in the field of healing.

Seven energy fields interpenetrate the human body. Each energy field has a different frequency, color, and function.

The human energy fields contain information, act purposefully, and are essential for life. They duplicate the biological, mental, emotional, and spiritual components of human beings and interact with them.

Each cell and organ of the physical body is duplicated by the first energy field, the energy blueprint, and interacts with it. When this energy field becomes defective or weak, we are programmed to become ill.

When healing energy is imparted, the energy fields are strengthened and transformed into healthy blueprints that are impressed upon the physical, mental, emotional, and spiritual components, creating health and wholeness.

The blueprint energy field radiates to one-fourth inch above the skin; the other energy fields go out further, with the seventh radiating out to twenty or more feet.

The role of consciousness is crucial to healing. A change in consciousness can result in the instant healing of any disease. Research has just begun in this area.

This working model becomes a bridge of understanding between healing and conventional medical models.

Chouhan's Research

In 1987, I met one of the world's leading healing researchers, Ramesh Chouhan, M.D., at a Montreal conference. He had just completed eight years of clinical studies at his JIPMER Hospital Bioelectrography Lab, Pondicherry, India, in which he had screened 25,000 women's health by studying their photographed fingertip energy fields. He discovered that cancer leaves a specific signature in the energy field that is detectable three to six months before its physical appearance in the body.

This research provides objective evidence that cancer begins in the human energy field, causing the cancer in the body. Heal the human energy field and physical cancer disappears.

But what causes the human energy field to become distorted with cancer? For years the suspected agent has been emotional pain. This would account for Jane's dramatic healing in Chapter One. Her cancer disappeared when the emotional pain was removed from her emotional energy field. With her emotional energy field healed, Jane bathed her physical body with healthy energy, curing her cancer.

Chouhan also discovered an energy field signature that precedes the physical onset of arthritis by six to twelve months. And the energy field of a woman changes in a characteristic way within an hour of conception.

The 1989 Chouhan-Weston Studies

I joined Dr. Chouhan at JIPMER Hospital as the healer in clinical studies designed to videotape the changes in the human energy fields during the healing encounter. The videotape evidence vividly pictured these objective truths:

Upon healing touch, the human blue energy field changes in two to three seconds to a white energy field about twice the baseline blue's size.

Further touch builds the needed amount or threshold of energy within the patient to a healing level. This was eighty-nine seconds for a head cold, about ten minutes for cancer, and three sessions over forty-eight hours for chronic spinal pain.

PROGRESS OF BLUEPRINT ENERGY FIELD PROGRAMMED DISEASE

18-24 MONTHS BEFORE ONSET OF DISEASE, the blueprint energy field becomes distressed by emotional trauma.

3-12 MONTHS BEFORE ONSET OF DISEASE, the blueprint energy field becomes distorted by emotional pain and develops the energy signature of a disease. This sends signals, telling the physical body to become diseased.

0 MONTHS — PRODUCE ONSET OF DISEASE SYMPTOMS, as the emotionally distorted blueprint energy field reaches a quantitative threshold that overwhelms the body's immune system. The qualities of emotional pain, the personality of the subject, and genetic predisposition determine the type of disease.

INTERVENTION. The removal of emotional pain at any point in this process produces a healthy blueprint energy field that signals the physical body to be well. The earlier the intervention, the more rapidly the healing takes place. The easiest way to permanently remove emotional pain is through Emotional Release Therapy.

EARLY DETECTION. Bioelectrography can detect the disease signature in the blueprint energy field for diseases such as cancer and arthritis before the physical onset of the disease.

Healing touch on only the forehead and nape of the neck was transmitted into the fingertips, into the spine, into the genitals, and into the toes. Holding only one hand produced the same results.

Qualities of Healing Energy

Here are some scientifically verified facts about healing energy.

- Healing energy is scientifically visible, emerging from the palms of the hands and finger pads.
- Healing energy is attuned to the specific frequency of plus or minus 7.83 hertz.
- Applied to the ill, healing-charged water, cotton, wool, and surgical gauze produce the same outcomes as healing hands.
- Healing energy is extremely stable. Stored for two years, healing-charged bottled water does not diminish in strength, making it the most stable known form of stored energy. This is also a quality of holy relics and places, and of healing spas. Sunlight and temperatures above the water boiling point diminish it.
- Healing energy diminishes quickly when transmitted to ill living organisms. Like an antibiotic, healing energy acts as a process and must be maintained at a therapeutic level by repeated transmissions.
- Trained healers can emit more than 200 volts of healing energy. If you generate only one volt, you emit a billion times more voltage than the human brain, enough to clearly heal effectively. This may be why spiritual healing is able to normalize the brainwave patterns of the ill.

- The intentions of the toucher become encoded in the information of the transmitted energy.
- Healing energy can prevent an anticipated disease from occurring.
- Healing energy produces the optimum conditions for life.
- Healing energy increases the amount of oxygen in the blood by up to twelve percent for about twenty-four hours.

This scientific picture helps us use healing touch more intelligently. It also gives us more confidence in practicing it upon ourselves.

PART TWO:

HEALING YOUR EMOTIONS

(An Essential Step)

6

The Mind-Body Connection

Could psychological factors cause you to need an illness?

What, if any, psychological factors have contributed to your medical condition?

For decades, we have heard the word *psychosomatic*. When a physician heard a patient's complaints and diagnostic tests revealed no disease, the doctor would say the condition was psychosomatic or psychological in nature.

Psychoneuroimmunology

The medical term *psychoimmunology*, the first term used to describe the mind-body connection, was coined in 1966 by psychiatrist George Solomon of the University of Southern California. It was later expanded to the term used today, *psychoneuroimmunology*.

Intriguing psychoneuroimmunological evidence now exists showing that psychological factors directly affect recovery from cancer, heart disease, colds, asthma, ulcers, migraine headaches, and broken bones.

Not only do psychological factors directly affect recovery in our healing model, but psychological factors are a direct cause of most diseases. Most of what we mean by psychological factors is the presence of emotional pain, such as stress, anger, anxiety, fear, or depression. The clinical studies suggest that emotional pain distorts the human energy fields before the onset of disease.

Some twenty years ago, studies showed that a painful loss often preceded the onset of cancer by twelve to eighteen months. If a person resolved the emotional hurt, no cancer developed. All this fits together as an understandable pattern.

Some Reasons for Needing an Illness

In the following chapters, you will be introduced to Emotional Release Therapy. It will help you get well by helping you release your emotional hurts. But if you are at some level choosing to be ill or to die, you might not choose to release your emotional hurts. In order to get well, you must decide that you want to live. You must realize the consequences of refusing to change: continuing illness leading to further suffering and possible death.

You must learn to take charge of your life. Taking charge means making the needed changes that will bring you ongoing happiness and satisfaction. In the process, you may need to overcome some of the following reasons for needing an illness.

- When you are trapped in ongoing unhappiness at home and at work, at some level you may choose illness and death as the only perceived way out.

- Childhood emotional, physical, or sexual abuse may be the root cause of adult misery and failure, all contributing to illness.

- Abandonment, divorce, or emotional hurts from a previous relationship can cause life-long emotional pain and illness.

- Unresolved guilt, grief, or anger following a tragedy may give rise to illness as self-punishment.

- Stress and bitterness due to the long-term care of a now-deceased loved one can cause life-threatening illnesses that offer an escape from despair.

- The illness of one family member may serve a dysfunctional family's needs. Families may unknowingly seek to maintain the illness of a member because it meets another family member's needs.

- Illness can be a means of manipulating loved ones, including permitting the ill person to be dependent and cared for, or keeping a family member from leaving home.

- We can use an illness to punish those with whom we are angry, including ourselves.

- Illness can represent an escape from boredom and the loss of meaning and self-worth. Such illnesses can occur when children leave home, when one retires, or as a result of poverty or unemployment.

- A distorted or faulty life script may cause us to believe that illness and death will come at a certain age because it happened that way to other family members.

If you recognize yourself in these or similar situations, then you may be able to escape both illness and death by choosing life. Staying where we are is usually a matter of free choice. We are responsible for our own health and life, and we have the power to influence our circumstances.

Your present emotional pain may be trapping you, making you unable to think clearly enough to escape your present psychological state. Detour in your reading and thoroughly use Chapter 8 to release your emotional hurts and your present fixated emotional state. Then return to this chapter with a clear mind, to explore the possible psychological roots of your present condition. You will also be returning with the abundant energy needed to fight for your health and your life.

7

The Basis Of Emotional Pain

Why can't we easily shake off emotional pain?

Why can emotional hurts be just as painful to us years later as when they first occurred?

The answers to these questions grow from our understanding of the role of human energy fields. Emotional pain is stored in our emotional energy field and not in our physical brains. For that reason, no matter how hard we think and think and think, we cannot resolve our emotional pain. Only through our feelings do we have access to the emotional energy field. That is also why most self-help approaches do not work; they are based upon thinking approaches that have no access to the emotional energy field.

Every unresolved emotional pain we have ever experienced is stored in our emotional energy fields. They are alive and stored as bits of hurt. Positive emotions are also present in the emotional energy field. In fact, all emotional states are stored there, each influenced by past unresolved emotional pain. Negative and positive emotions war within us for dominance.

The stored unresolved emotional pains influence our thinking, decisions, actions, personalities, and ability to cope with life. They are the cause of destructive moods and behaviors. They can also cause distortions in the blueprint energy field that maintains our physical health. These energy field distortions then become the major cause of physical disease.

Conventional medicine can usually intervene and restore the physical body to health, temporarily restoring the blueprint energy field. But we remain vulnerable to disease as long as unresolved emotional pain keeps distorting our energy fields.

Like Being Possessed

Having emotional pain is like being possessed. Emotional pain has a life of its own beyond our conscious mental control. No matter how we try to shake it off, it clings to us like glue.

Most of us learn ways to wall it off more or less or suppress it from our conscious awareness. Doing so is a necessary normal defense to protect us from emotional overload.

Some manage emotional pain by closing themselves to all awareness of feelings. Such closing-off means living only in the thinking mode, so that you have no contact with your emotional self. Some of us are better at this than others. Some fail to suppress successfully and are haunted daily by their hurts.

No matter how well you cope, however, unresolved emotional pain remains destructive. It can seep through your defenses as nameless anxiety, fear, stress, anger, or depression. Even when you cannot feel them, destructive emotions can distort your blueprint energy field.

Unhealed emotional pain causes diseases that are resistant to both conventional medical care and alternative medical care. As long as the blueprint energy field is distorted by the hurts in the emotional energy field, a constant signal is being sent to the physical body to be ill.

(The Most Important Aspect of Healing . . .)

8

Healing Emotional Pain

How would you like to release all your emotional hurts and destructive emotional states, ending up feeling a sense of inner peace and contentment?

How would you like to wake up each morning feeling happy and joyous about being alive?

How would you like to get well and become completely healthy and whole?

How would you like to be freed from the emotional barriers that have sabotaged your efforts at meeting personal goals and finding your true self?

These are the amazing promises of Emotional Release Therapy.

Emotional Release Therapy is an entirely new tool for removing painful memories. It also removes existing troubling emotional states such as anxiety and anger, fear and depression. This has never before been possible. This is a wonderful new discovery.

It may be your key to renewed health and longevity. For when you experience ongoing inner peace and contentment, your energy fields return to health, producing health in your physical body.

The results of Emotional Release Therapy are similar to results from surgery. In surgery diseased tissue is removed, leaving only healthy tissue. Emotional Release Therapy does not use a scalpel. Instead, diseased or painful emotions are released into your hand, leaving only healthy emotions behind.

Emotional Release Therapy is revolutionary in scope. It will radically alter the way in which health care is practiced. Millions of people will now be able to live happy and productive lives following just one or more therapy sessions. This prospect is only a small part of the Emotional Release Therapy story.

The Yearning Runs Deep

In June 1996, I met an elderly woman while working in a pranic healing center in Bangalore, India. She had expressed no interest in her daughter's healing work, but when her daughter told her about the American who could remove painful memories from throughout a lifetime, she said, "I want to see this Dr. Weston tomorrow."

The next morning, eighty-two-year old Mala walked into the healing center. She was stooped over, the weight of a lifetime etched upon her lined face. For seventy-five minutes, she silently released her long history of emotional pain into my hand from her heart. I was amazed by the intensity of her release.

When Mala finished, she arose and stood straight. I knew her deepest yearnings had been fulfilled, for her face looked peaceful and many years younger. Then she simply stated, "I feel wonderful!" This is the miracle of Emotional Release Therapy.

All Emotional Pain

Try to release all painful memories, hurts, or emotional states. Afterwards, you will still be able to honestly feel and express any emotion, and will likely be even more capable of doing so than before. Especially, do not hold on to rage or anger. Determine to let them go.

You may choose to delay the release of some painful emotions. For sixteen months, my sister nursed her husband through brain cancer. After his death, I observed her grief, exhaustion, and despair for a month before cautiously offering her Emotional Release Therapy. She eagerly accepted my offer, as if I should have offered it sooner. Within days, she was her old energetic, optimistic self. As a widow, she still had the difficult task of rebuilding her life, but was now more capable of doing it.

No strong emotional pain should be held for long, for it will eventually make you ill and can literally kill you.

Many Ways To Do It

The diversity of ways in which minds operate means that you must find a way that works for you. Some people easily visualize mental images; some do not. Some people are in touch with their feelings, while thinking predominates in others. You will be offered a way that works for you.

You Must Release *Emotions*

Your emotions are stored in your emotional energy field. Releasing *thoughts* of hurts cannot release the hurts.

You must release *emotions*. Your ability to feel determines the ease with which you will release your hurts.

Children can release a lifetime of hurts within ten minutes. Feeling-type women will take thirty to sixty minutes for the initial release. Thinking-type men will likely take longer. But thinking types will be provided suitable ways.

Everyone has painful memories and troubling emotional states. Some are buried so deeply that it may take extra work—and several sessions—to release them. Usually, recalled traumatic pain will be released and gone forever, so it is worth the effort to be free at last.

The Role of Symbols

Feelings are fleeting, so it is difficult to hold onto any recalled feeling long enough to release it. We overcome this barrier by using symbols or images to represent the emotion. When you release your chosen symbol, you will also be releasing the intended emotion or event.

Symbols have the power and reality of what they represent. So you need to use a symbol to represent the emotions that you wish to release. To attach an emotion to a symbol, you must be able to recall how that emotion feels for a few seconds. To do so, go back to a time when you strongly experienced that emotion. Relive the feeling and attach it to your chosen symbol.

You can use any symbol that works for you. The most usable symbol has been a color. You choose a color to represent the emotion you wish to release. Men tend to choose black, purple, or red. Women tend to choose shades of blue, green, orange, yellow, brown, and red.

Any color works. Other symbols work as well. You can use any object that you can visualize as your symbol and release into your hand.

Visualizing is best done by not trying hard. Relax by taking two deep breaths. Try a color and see if you can gently hold that color in your mind. Black is the easiest to use. If the color changes in practice or while doing the real thing, go with the new color.

If you cannot visualize, go to the emotion or traumatic event you wish to release. Try to release it as you relive it.

Practicing Emotional Release Therapy

Find a dimly lit, quiet place where you will not be disturbed, even by the phone. Find a comfortable place to lie down on your back. Later, it can be done sitting.

Ask yourself:
a) Do I have an emotional hurt that haunts me every day of my life?
b) Do I daily dwell in any emotional state that makes me unhappy or sabotages my life?
c) Do I daily dwell in any emotional state that makes my loved ones unhappy?

Focus on your answers. These answers are the best place to begin.

Relax. Take two deep breaths. Relax your body by tensing every part of your body and then relaxing it. Then tell yourself, "As I count from ten to one, every muscle in my body will relax more with each count." Inhale deeply and on each exhale count down, beginning with ten.

Your hand. Begin by placing your flattened dominant hand (right- or left-handedness) over your heart. Your hand is capable of receiving the energy your heart releases and will later fill your heart with spiritual blessings.

A symbol. Choose the emotion or event that causes your worst pain. Choose a color or object as a symbol for releasing your chosen emotion. Feel the emotion you are about to release. Visualize your symbol and place it in your heart area. Offer a prayer that expresses your intentions.

Using Emotional Release Therapy on yourself works well. You will feel little heat and it takes up to thirty seconds to feel it entering your hand.

Prayer.

God, I no longer want this emotional pain and I choose to release it. As I release this symbol into my hand, I release the emotion it represents. I lovingly receive the emotion into my hand and then release it into your eternal care. Thank you. Amen.

Release. Release the symbol into your hand. View your hand as a magnet or a vacuum, pulling your emotion into itself. Or let the color flow like a river into your hand. Or invent your own release mechanism. There may be a one-to-three minute delay before you feel heat or energy entering your hand. Once you learn to do this exercise, try to feel the emotion, letting it flow into your hand with the color. If the color changes, go with the new color.

Checking your progress. If the emotional release is working for you, you will be aware of an energy or heat entering your hand. That is the emotion you are releasing.

Shake off the heat. When your hand grows very warm, shake it to remove the heat of your release. This shaking is necessary because your hand quickly fills to capacity with released emotional heat. By shaking it, you are emptying it so it can receive more emotional heat. Shaking it also makes your hand more sensitive, so that you can feel the heat release stop. When this happens, you have completed the release of that specific emotion. Then you can move on to another emotion. Now place your hand back on your heart.

CAUTION. When releasing anger, fear, depression, or enormous trauma, you might store the emotional release in your arms or legs. You would know this because these limbs become heavy or weak. To avoid this tissue storage, place a bowl of salted water beside you. Rather than shaking your hand, dip it in the salt water, releasing the emotional pain into the salt water. Or do the Emotional Release Therapy outside. Your feet will release the emotional pain into Earth. Or, afterwards, take an hour salt-water bath, using five cups of salt. Rock salt or water softener salt is the cheapest. Make sure the salt is chemical-free.

A tingling. If you feel a tingling in your hand, you are releasing thoughts, not feelings. Reach deeper for your emotions.

Nothing. If you feel nothing entering your hand, start over. This time, try releasing the emotion or event directly into your hand. If needed, try releasing the emotion with each exhale.

Still nothing. If you still feel no energy or heat entering your hand, do not give up. Take a break and start over again from the beginning. You learned some insights in your first attempt. Everyone eventually succeeds.

Finished. You have finished releasing your initial emotion from your heart when no further heat or energy enters your hand or when your color symbol lightens or turns white.

Proceed to other releases. Keep releasing in this manner until you have released what you need to release.

Proceed to the abdomen. Now move your hand to your abdomen (just below your navel) and repeat the procedure. It is here that gut-level emotions such as fear and anger tend to gather. If you feel no release, no emotions are store there.

Then to the diaphragm. When finished with the abdomen, move your hand to your diaphragm (just below the ribs) to release any remaining emotional pain. Rarely will you feel a release, but do this step anyway, just in case.

Poor self-image. Place your hand on your heart. Choose a color. Release the feelings concerning anything you do not like about yourself. This might include your face, other body parts, your personality, your character, your style, your laugh, etc.

Buried Emotions. Now use a hypnotism technique to recover buried emotions. Do not try to do anything; just flow passively with what is happening. Tell yourself, *On the count of three, I will release the emotional pain that is causing my present medical condition [or unhappiness]. One, two, three, release.* You are likely to feel a rush of heat or energy entering your hand.

Cutting ties. If you have people in your past or present who cause you emotional pain, cutting your energy ties to them can stop the pain. For each person, visualize a cord of energy connecting you to him or her. Then, take an imaginary pair of scissors and cut this connecting cord to sever any energy contact with them. While doing so, pray, "God, I cut this cord that binds me to _____. May his/her energy no longer have an effect upon me. Thank you. Amen."

Closing prayer. Close each session with a sacred blessing. With your hand on your heart, pray: *God, where I have removed emotions and left emptiness, fill me with your love, joy and peace. Thank you. Amen.*

Hand. Leave your hand on your heart for at least a minute, for your hand is acting for God in filling you with these sacred qualities. If you do not do so, you will be left feeling an uncomfortable emptiness. This also protects you from the return of any negative emotions.

Future Therapy Sessions

In future sessions, continue your release of painful memories. Even though you are not now aware of the pain, go back to every moment in your life when you felt hurt, rejection, failure, fear, anger, grief, etc. You will feel energized by your efforts.

Unknown emotional fixations. Go through every possible emotion to find if you might secretly possess a hidden reservoir of it that you can release. These emotional barriers sabotage your best efforts for interpersonal harmony, personal growth, empowerment, and success. After releasing unknown fear for twenty minutes, I was rewarded with a deep sense of inner serenity and a burst of energy.

Emotions to uncover and release include:

anger	fear	pessimism
anxiety	grief	sadness
depression	guilt	shyness
doubt	inadequacy	stress
envy	jealousy	worry
failure	negativity	performance anxieties

Now, go in your new freedom to grow and become your true self and be joyously happy.

Where To Go from Here

If you have been unable to release your emotional pain, Chapter 10 offers you another possibility.

9

Coping With a Scary Diagnosis

You may have worked through the emotional shock of a scary diagnosis during Chapter 8 or at some earlier time. Still, have the patience to explore this chapter. You need to be sure that denial is not blocking your ability to plan clearly.

From the moment you receive a frightening medical diagnosis, the emotional issues begin overshadowing the physical symptoms. You now feel trapped in an unreliable body with no way out. The emotional shock of diagnosis can hinder or block the effects of the best medical care, Emotional Release Therapy, or self-healing touch prayer.

Facing a health crisis is one of the most frightening experiences of your life. Your emotional responses are predictable. You are not only physically sick; you have been emotionally wounded. Your willingness to realize that you have been emotionally impaired by the diagnosis opens you to making that emotional pain a top priority for self-healing.

I wrote the following prayer to express myself following my life-threatening heart attack:

A Prayer in the Midst of an Illness

God, I am puzzled by what has happened to me. My life has abruptly changed. My plans have been interrupted. My confidence has been shattered and my peace destroyed. I am angry. I am hurt. I am frightened. I am not sure I can face tomorrow, yet I really have no choice, for today is here and tomorrow comes. Who will deliver me from this endless nightmare? You, God? Are you my strength and my salvation?

I feel as if somehow I have failed. I feel guilty about being sick when I truly wish to be well. I am proud. I have always considered myself to be so competent and self-reliant and yet now I feel so helpless. Enable me to accept the loving care of those who love me. Hold me in your love. I seem to be dwelling more and more with you, God. You are becoming my strength and my salvation.

God, remove my anger, my hurt, my fear, my loss, my darkness, as I seek to dwell in you. Fill my soul with your transforming light. Hold me in your never-failing strong arms and never let me go! Yes! You have become my strength and my salvation!

I often feel sad. Will I ever run again, with the breeze caressing my face? Will I ever dance again, with vibrant life coursing through my veins? Will I ever laugh without a bitter edge? Will I ever sing with joy filling my soul? Will I ever be loved again because I am strong and whole? Lord, God, please heal my inner being and fill me with your strength, with the love, joy, and peace of your presence. For you, God, are my strength and my salvation!

God, I often ponder the death of my dreams. I have struggled and have grown. I have laughed and I have played. I have created and achieved. I have loved and known deep love. I have dreamed of many years down the road. I once thought earthly life was endless, but now I know that each earthly journey is limited. Open me to new dreams that will still yield happiness and fulfillment. Teach me the joys of this day. For you are my strength and my salvation!

God, assure me that my soul is eternal. Let me live in your love, that when this earthly journey ends, with trust, I will gladly rest in your everlasting arms . . . free to grow and to become forever. I know that you are with me in life, in death, and in life beyond death. For you are my strength and my salvation!

God, help me to see clearly through new eyes. Open me to the opportunities and joys still before me. You have enabled me to take control of my life. I choose to live each day fully and satisfyingly. I choose to live, to love, to care! I choose to live in your presence. Completely transform my inner being so that I am filled with love and light! Heal me in body, mind, and spirit that I might become a blessing to myself and to others. I know that new life awaits me. For you are my strength and my salvation! Amen.

The Battle of Crisis

Your first inner battle is brought on by the health crisis itself. Daily plans and responsibilities will probably need to be put on hold. Being acutely ill, hospitalized, or emotionally immobilized, or receiving a fear-inducing diagnosis, all call for refocusing your energies solely upon yourself. Life will momentarily have to go on without your contributions. Others will pick up the slack! You are far more important than any of your former responsibilities. Assert your determination to deal with your own immediate needs, because your survival depends upon it. Be selfish with loved ones. Your life depends upon it.

Perspective

Put your crisis in perspective. Most crises are accompanied by disruptions, pain, fear, confusion, and a sense of helplessness. These are not pleasant experiences but they are normal human reactions. If you are reading this, you survived. Even in life-threatening medical emergencies, ninety-eight percent survive the immediate crisis.

A health crisis can eventually be recognized as a friend. It may tell you that you are not happy or satisfied. It may begin an inner search for what needs to be healed within you, such as painful memories, emotional trauma, anger, fear, sadness, or a sense of personal inadequacy. It can change your vocational priorities, deepen your relationship with loved ones, or lead to a healthier lifestyle. It can lead to a closer relationship with God, transforming you into a stronger, wiser, more spiritual person.

The Battle with Fear

Fear is the reaction we deny most, but fear has a purpose. It warns us that something we regard highly is being threatened. In this case, it is life itself, as well as all that your life has been focused upon. Admitting fear lessens it. As a first step, admit to yourself that you are fearful.

If you are fearful, your loved ones are also likely to be fearful. Talk about your fear with them. It strengthens all of you.

The fear of dying and the fear of living are tied together. Once one conquers the fear of death, both fears end. Exploring the fear of dying involves several questions:

Do I have any regrets? If so, how do I make amends?

Has my life been worthwhile? If not, what can I do now to make myself feel worthwhile?

Is there anything I deeply desire to do, if I should need to face death? If so, can I still in some way accomplish it?

Do I really believe in the afterlife at the deepest emotional and spiritual levels? What assurances do I need in order to believe?

A Prayer for Releasing Fear

Before beginning, prepare for the Emotional Release Therapy that healed your emotional pain in Chapter 8. Place your dominant hand over your heart. Choose a color to symbolize your fear. Prepare to release your fear into your hand at the prayer cue. Now, pray:

> *God, I am filled with fear. I fear this illness. I fear the dramatic changes taking place in my life. I fear for my loved ones. I have fear about money matters. I fear for my ability to survive. I fear fear. I now choose to release my fear.*
>
> *God, I release my fear into my hand, using the color I have chosen, and then release it into your eternal care.*

Pause in this prayer and take all the time you need. Then, keep your hand on your heart and continue praying.

> *I have released my fear to you, God. I have placed myself in your loving hands. I accept your strength and your salvation. Let your love, your strength, your assurance, and your peace flow through my hand and into my heart.*

You are with me in life, in death, in life beyond death. Make me aware of my own sacred and eternal nature. Your power and presence course throughout me and dwell within me. Thank you, God. I rest in your care. Amen.

The Value of Hope

To hope is to have optimism about the future. Hope says that no matter how bad things are now, I will get better.

You bought this book out of a sense of hope, saying to yourself, "Maybe I can regain my health by using *Healing Yourself.*"

Alternative medicine offers clinical evidence that conditions unresponsive to conventional treatment may respond well to complementary approaches. This is a basis for realistic hope.

Hope also leads us to God. This book is based upon the belief that God is our hope and our salvation. Religious experiences provide us not only with a hope but also with an inner assurance that we are eternal. Death can come, not as an enemy to be feared, but as a peaceful transition into further growth and fulfillment, a final and beautiful healing.

A Prayer for Nurturing Hope

Before beginning, prepare for the Emotional Release Therapy that healed your emotional pain in Chapter 8. Place your dominant hand over your heart. Choose a color to symbolize your fear. Prepare to release your fear into your hand at the prayer cue. Now, pray:

God, there are moments when I am filled with doubt and pessimism about the course of my medical

*condition and my life. I now choose to release the
spirits of doubt and pessimism.*

*God, I release doubt and pessimism into my hand,
using the color I have chosen, and then release it into
your eternal care.*

Pause in this prayer and take all the time you need.
Then, keep your hand on your heart and continue praying.

*God, where my heart is now empty, let your sacred
hope flow through my hand and into my heart, filling
me with hope.*

*Be with me through all of my struggles, for I trust
you to guide and sustain me on my journey back to
health and wholeness. Amen.*

Five Strategies for Coping

People facing a health crisis naturally use five common strategies for reducing emotional pain. They are
unrehearsed responses to danger, but they are also
friends that protect us from overwhelming worry and
stress. These strategies are denial, anger, bargaining,
depression, and acceptance.

Although they are coping strategies, the first four
must be understood and successfully worked through,
so that we can reach the fifth—acceptance. Unresolved,
they can permit a disease to win without a fight. They
detour us from the more urgent task of combating the
disease.

These reactions do not occur in any specific order,
though acceptance usually comes last, if it comes at all.
Several or all may be occurring at one time. The following
understanding and self-healing prayers are designed to help
you work through these protective reactions.

1) Denial

Denial involves the emotional inability to either hear or accept the reality or dangers involved in a life-threatening medical diagnosis. Denial might say, "It's not serious. I do not need any medical treatment. I'll just continue living as I always have."

Early denial can be beneficial. Denial allows the medical truth to sink in slowly as one becomes emotionally able to handle it, one bit at a time. But denial can hold one in a hypnotic-like state where one is unable to see reality, even when others try to force it upon us. One way of working through denial is by sharing your fears with loved ones or a support group.

- What are my denials?
- What fears prompt them?
- What can I do to resolve those fears?

A Prayer for Releasing Denial

Before beginning, prepare for the Emotional Release Therapy that healed your emotional pain in Chapter 8. Place your dominant hand over your heart. Choose a color to symbolize your fear. Prepare to release your fear into your hand at the prayer cue. Now, pray:

> God, I have always been so self-reliant and competent. I had thought of myself as being strong and secure. Now I know fear and helplessness. There is no easy way out. There is no quick fix. This new journey is difficult. As I seek to handle it, let the truth slowly sink in. Provide me with the hope that I can handle all that is before me. Enable me to make the changes I need to fight for my health and my life.

> *God, I release any denial I have about the serious-*
> *ness of my illness into my hand, using the color I have*
> *chosen, and then release it into your eternal care.*

Pause in this prayer and take all the time you need. Then, keep your hand on your heart and continue praying.

> *God, where my heart is now empty, let your sacred*
> *peace flow through my hand and into my heart, filling*
> *me with your peace.*

> *God, I need you now as never before. Strengthen*
> *my inner self with your presence and power. Assure*
> *me of your love. Fill me with your peace. Grant me*
> *wholeness in body, mind, and spirit, for you are*
> *becoming my strength and my salvation. Amen.*

2) Anger

Anger is always present, even when suppressed and denied. Anger is the direct response to the illness. It is the result of life being disrupted and endangered, of fear, of frustration, of moral indignation. Anger is seldom directed at the illness causing it. The anger is often inappropriately directed at family and friends, medical personnel, the hospital, God, religion, and clergy. Anger can become a mindless rage that alienates caregivers, thereby further isolating the ill.

Now, express your anger by saying to yourself, *I am really angry about my illness and what it is doing to me.* Drop your pretensions of being too mature for anger and make the same statement to a loved one. Then discuss your anger. This helps heal anger. Then ask yourself:

Am I angry because my whole life has been threatened and interrupted?

Am I angry with myself for a destructive lifestyle that may have contributed to my illness? Can I forgive myself?

Have I been misplacing my anger onto loved ones?

Can I now begin focusing my anger on my disease?

If so, vocally express this by saying: *I am angry with my medical condition and will fight to regain my health.*

A Prayer for Releasing Anger

Before beginning, prepare for the Emotional Release Therapy that healed your emotional pain in Chapter 8. Place your dominant hand over your heart. Choose a color to symbolize your anger. Prepare to release your anger into your hand at the prayer cue. Now, pray:

God, I am very angry. My medical condition has upset me. I am angry about being ill. My life has been rudely interrupted. It isn't fair! All the changes have made me irritable. This is a scary experience. I just want to blame someone for all the pain and change. I know the doctor wants the best for me. I know my loved ones have been trying to help me. I know that you, God, are not responsible for my illness. You want me to be healthy and whole.

God, I now release my anger into my hand, using the color I have chosen, and then release it into your eternal care.

Pause in this prayer and take all the time you need. Then, keep your hand on your heart and continue praying.

God, where my heart is now empty, let your sacred peace now flow through my hand and into my heart, filling me with your peace. Thank you, God. Now, help me to responsibly take charge of my life. Amen.

3) Bargaining

Bargaining is used to seek a way out. Bargaining is partially based upon guilt about being ill. It involves the belief that if I become a better person, I will somehow magically be blessed with health. Bargaining asks anyone we think has power—God, the universe, the family, a doctor, or the self—for one more chance to become well, in exchange for changing and leading a better life. It states, *If you will let me become well, I will do this . . . .* This promise assumes that becoming well is related to moral goodness, religious commitment, or a better lifestyle.

Bargaining is based upon magical thinking. It can increase our hope but it does not cure disease on its own. If bargaining is based upon the realistic hope that I can get well by using the best of conventional medicine, adopting a healthier lifestyle, and using Emotional Release Therapy and spiritual healing, then make an appropriate bargain.

A Bargaining Prayer

God, I would do almost anything to become well again. So, I want to bargain for my life, knowing that if I follow all of my options, I might just get well.

So, from this moment on I intend taking charge of my life. I am going to do whatever I need to do to find happiness and satisfaction in my personal life and in my work. Daily, I am going to pursue a healthier lifestyle. I am going to use the best of conventional medicine, and practice self-healing through Emotional Release Therapy and spiritual healing.

I forgive everyone who has ever hurt me and, at this moment, let go of any hurts inflicted by others. I forgive myself for the hurts I have inflicted upon others and will seek to make amends. I forgive myself for the guilt I am feeling about being ill. I let go of my anger, my hurts, and my fears. I will seek to create happiness and satisfaction within my life. I accept your healing power into my life. Thank you. Amen.

4) Depression

Depression is a normal part of a health crisis. A health crisis involves physical, emotional, and mental shock. One's whole life has been changed. There is sadness and grief over the many losses. Unexpressed or unresolved anger can result in depression.

Our sense of self-worth suffers. Often, we see ourselves as useless burdens to both others and ourselves. Illness can deepen our sense of failure in life, resulting in feelings of guilt and a deeper sense of personal inadequacy.

Surgical recovery is often followed by short-term depression. Returning home from a hospital stay can produce depression as the stresses at home take their toll.

The symptoms of depression are often delayed. We may do a marvelous job of coping with an illness only to find depression overwhelming us months after the initial crisis is over. Emotional and physical shock can traumatize the human energy fields. They may become torn and unable to maintain needed energy levels.

The symptoms of depression may include an emotional flatness, too much or too little sleep, lack of interest in food, gain or loss of weight, lack of energy, emotional darkness and heaviness, negativity and pessimism, bitterness, and an absence of appreciation for the care given by others. During depression, the brain tells us convincing lies that distort reality. These lies paint everything in the most convincingly negative terms.

Those who have been close to God usually find that their ability to sense God is severely diminished. A health care professional should be consulted when your depression is deep or accompanied by suicidal thoughts or destructive anger.

Most depression is self-limiting, disappearing as mysteriously as it began. Depression can be faced by accepting it as a normal human reaction to shock and loss. It can be diminished by appropriately expressing your anger at the illness and taking responsibility for your own life. It is helpful to go through the motions of seeking happiness and satisfaction. Do your best to love and care for those around you.

A Prayer for Releasing Depression

Before beginning, prepare for the Emotional Release Therapy that healed your emotional pain in Chapter 8. Place your dominant hand over your heart. Choose a color to symbolize your depression. Prepare to release your depression into your hand at the prayer cue. Now, pray:

God, life seems so bleak and useless right now. I do not have any energy and do not have much ambition. I am really feeling down. Even as I pray, I do not sense your presence. I know that I am sacred and precious but they are just words right now. I know that my life has been worthwhile, full of many wonderful people and experiences, much happiness and joy.

God, all I can do is affirm the goodness of life and try to hold on until the darkness is replaced by your marvelous light and love. Help me to spot the lies that my depressed emotions are telling me. Life is good. I am good. You are good. My loved ones love me. Life will be beautiful again.

God, I now release my depression into my hand, using the color I have chosen, and then release it into your eternal care.

Pause in this prayer and take all the time you need. Then, keep your hand on your heart and continue praying.

God, where my heart is now empty, let your sacred peace and hope flow through my hand and into my heart, filling me with your presence. Thank you, God.

God, it feels so good to feel light and whole once more. I rejoice in your healing power. Amen.

5) Acceptance

Acceptance of one's illness or possible death is not resignation. Acceptance emerges from the struggles surrounding one's condition and represents a growing maturity. I find acceptance can best be attained through the spiritual journey with God. Many people report that acceptance was the first step in their journey back to wholeness. Acceptance permits focus and intention to come alive.

An illness contains many positive messages, making it a friend in disguise. It may be a helpful warning message that one's life is focused upon the wrong priorities. When you reach the acceptance stage, you will know that you have grown wiser. You will rejoice in the new person who is emerging.

Acceptance is not resignation, passivity, or depression. It is making peace with your situation. It is the result of conquering fear, coming to terms with anger, and coping with despair.

A Prayer of Acceptance

God, this is the most difficult struggle of my life. I do not want this illness. If I had a choice, I would be well. This is so unfair in many ways. I cannot escape this physical body of mine. I can see no easy way out. I am angry, frightened, and indignant at what is happening to me. I am not sure I can adjust. Some days I live as if nothing has happened. On other days, reality hits me squarely and I hurt.

God, give me the strength and wisdom to accept what has happened to me and to alter my life accordingly. Enable me to see my life as worthwhile and meaningful. Help me to celebrate the joys that I have known and the fulfillment still before me. Help me to live each day as happily as possible and to awaken each morning with the words, "Thank you God for another day." Provide me with the wisdom I need to get my life together. Grant me your presence and peace. Thank you. Amen.

10

Emotional Release Therapy

These are the wonderful benefits of practicing Emotional Release Therapy on other people:

You can ask a loved one to practice it upon you. Have that person read Chapter 8 before reading this chapter.

You can help others release their painful memories and fixated negative emotional states, giving them happiness and health.

You can help troubled children. The experiential evidence suggests that emotional hurts cause attention deficit disorder, behavioral problems, allergies, and chronic and life-threatening illnesses. Emotional Release Therapy can heal all emotional, physical, and interpersonal childhood traumas.

You can help seemingly insensitive persons get in touch with their feelings so that they can become emotionally more sensitive, compassionate and nurturing.

You can experience deep spiritual bliss while practicing Emotional Release Therapy.

Practicing Emotional Release Therapy with Others

Having read Chapter 8, you already have a thorough understanding of Emotional Release Therapy. Therefore, we will quickly move into the directions for practicing it with others.

You are the therapist and the person you are helping is referred to as your client. During actual practice, you will, of course, address each other by name.

You do not need to know the nature of your client's emotional pain to be effective.

In your own words, tell your client what Emotional Release Therapy can do. Basically, you can release any painful memory or destructive emotional state into the hand on your chest. It will be completely gone.

Seating. Sit beside your client on a couch or on upright chairs, facing the side of your client so that your dominant hand can touch his or her chest. It is helpful to use a chair with armrests to support your arm so it will not become too tired for your hand to remain in place. Aching arms are the most difficult part of the practice.

The color. Tell your client to choose a color that will be a symbol that represents his or her emotional hurt. Tell your client if the color changes, go with the new color.

Place your hand. Ask permission to touch: "May I place my hand above your heart on your sternum?" Now place your dominant hand on the sternum, the bony area above the heart.

Pray. Say *"Let us pray,"* then offer this prayer: *God, _____ has chosen to release his/her emotional hurts into my hand using the symbol of the chosen color. I lovingly receive the color into my hand and release it into your eternal care. Thank you. Amen.*

Feel the emotion. Tell your client, "Now release the color into my hand. When you can do that, choose an emotional pain you wish to release and release it into the color. I will feel your release into my hand as a heat energy. I will tell you when you are doing it."

Hand image. Tell your client, "Think of my hand as a magnet drawing the pain into it, or let the color flow into my hand like a river of water, or use your imagination and do your own thing."

Coaching. When you feel heat entering your hand, encourage your client by saying, "I feel the heat of your emotional release entering my hand. Whatever you are doing, keep doing. It is working." This encouraging feedback gives your client confidence. The result is a sharp increase of the heat entering your hand.

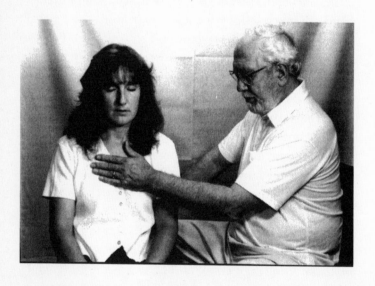

Both persons are comfortable in this basic position.

A tingling or nothing. If you feel a tingling, your client is releasing thoughts rather than emotions. If you feel nothing, your client is releasing nothing. In either case, change tactics. Coach your client to feel more deeply and directly release emotions. Here is how: First, tell your client what you are feeling in your hand and what that means. Second, continue by telling your client, "Feel your emotional pain, then say to yourself, 'I no longer need this pain and I choose to release it directly into the hand on my chest." If this does not work, take a break and start over again from the beginning. Having learned from their first experience, clients usually can do it on a second try.

Hand shaking. Your hand can hold only so much emotional heat. About once a minute, remove your hand, shake off the heat, and return it to the chest. Doing so takes only seconds. Afterwards, your hand can receive more emotional heat. It can also better sense the flow of heat from the client.

Finishing a release. A time will come when the client will have completely released the emotion he has been working on. After a shaking of it, you will feel this when you sense no heat entering your hand. You then tell your client, "I no longer feel heat entering my hand. You can now move onto another emotion you wish to release." Keep repeating this process.

Your mind. Keep your own mind in a quiet and peaceful state. Sometimes visualize your hand drawing the painful emotion into it. Pray for your client's success. You may find yourself feeling deeply spiritual. You will find yourself being patient and content, even for an hour.

After a time. Say to your client, "Take all the time you need. When you think you are finished, tell me." After he or she does so, proceed.

Further coaching. If you sense your client may have missed a needed release, this is the time to suggest that release. I often ask my clients at this time to individually release fear, anger, and depression. If they have already done so, they will tell you.

Irritating loved ones. "Think about your loved ones. If one of them does something that is irritating or annoying, release it into my hand."

Client's self-image. "Is there anything about yourself you do not like, such as body parts, personality, character, style? Release the feelings attached to these images."

Using suggestion. Say, "We are going deeply into your hidden emotional pain. I want you to relax and just let this happen. When I have counted to three, you will immediately release all the buried painful emotions that are hurting you. One, two, three. Now release." You will usually feel a large surge of energy or heat enter your hand.

The closing blessing. At this moment, your client may be feeling uncomfortably empty. Let your hand on his or her sternum fill the gaps in his or her emotional energy field with sacred qualities. Pray, *"God, fill ____ with your love and peace, your joy and presence. Thank you. Amen."* Let your hand remain in place for a minute.

Abdominal storage. Now ask the client's permission to place your hand on his or her abdomen, just below the navel. Here you may find residual gut emotions such as anger, fear, and anxiety. Now repeat the Emotional

Release process you used on the sternum. This process usually takes only five minutes. A few people need up to fifteen minutes. When you finish here, offer another prayer blessing.

You have now completed your first session of Emotional Release Therapy. Your client should be able to continue further sessions on his or her own. Suggest that your client read Chapter 8.

CAUTION: Physical Impairment Is Possible

If you practice Emotional Release Therapy regularly with others, you may begin storing the released painful emotions of others within the tissue of your own body. The symptoms of doing so are a heaviness in your legs, with your calves aching when you walk, or the weakening of the arm of your dominant hand.

There are three solutions for this. Use one of them.

- Before practicing Emotional Release Therapy, add table salt to a bowl of water large enough to place your hand in. Place this saltwater solution next to you. Rather than shake the heat off your hands, quickly dip it in the saltwater solution. Have a dishtowel handy. This takes only about three seconds.

- Ground yourself to Earth during Emotional Release Therapy. Practice it with your stocking on grass or grounded concrete. Or place a grounding wire around your ankle and ground it to the ground in the electrical receptacle, or the cold water pipe, or into the ground outside your door.

- Bathe your body in a saltwater bath once or twice a month. The salt water removes the painful emotional energy, also known as diseased bioplasma, from your own human energy fields. Add five cups of salt to a bathtub of water. Water softener salt with no chemical additives is the cheapest source of salt. It takes about twenty minutes for this salt to dissolve.

11

Healing Children

Children are easily wounded emotionally. These emotional wounds can then become permanently embedded in the emotional energy field throughout their lives, forever hampering their emotional, physical, mental, spiritual, and interpersonal growth and health.

Emotional Release with Pre-School Children

Jim. A member of my church told me this story about her second child. From the moment of his birth, he was a problem child. Jim had colic, diaper rash, crying tantrums, and irregular sleep patterns. At times, Jim's mother became so fatigued and angry that she had to fight her strong urge to throw him at a wall.

Then, a miracle occurred. At six months, Jim was baptized by my sacred touch upon his head. His mother reported that from that moment on, Jim was normal. No more colic, diaper rash, or crying tantrums. And he adopted a normal sleep pattern. Emotional healing can occur during any sacred touch.

It is likely that Jim became a problem child when he was somehow emotionally wounded, sometime between his conception and his first few weeks of life.

When To Do It

Practice Emotional Release Therapy on children with birth defects, with emotional trauma or hurts, with behavioral problems, with developmental problems, and with any disease.

How to Practice with Pre-School Children

Hand. Place your dominant hand, flattened straight, on his or her heart while you are next to the awake or sleeping child who may be sitting on your lap or lying down.

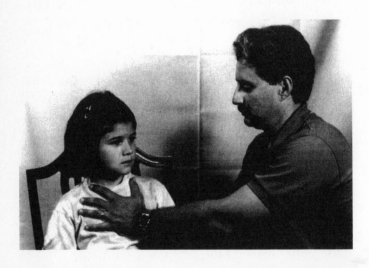

Children not only cooperate well but exhibit amazement, pleasure, and curiosity with what they are experiencing.

Color. Choose a color to symbolize the child's possible hurts.

Unity. Love the child and seek to be one with him or her. Do so until you feel merged with the child.

Trauma. Imagine the physical and emotional traumas that the child may have suffered. These include physical pain, anger, fear, and rejection.

Feel. With each specific situation, feel what the child might have felt.

Release. Now release each hurt into your hand by letting your chosen color flow from his or her heart into your hand. Receive the hurt into your hand. You will feel the heat or the energy of the hurt entering your hand. Each time it stops, begin releasing another possible hurt.

Bless. When the release is finished, keep your hand on the child's heart and fill him or her with God's spirit by praying: *God, use my hand to fill _____ with your love and light, your peace and joy. Thank you. Amen.* Leave your hand there for about a minute.

Afterwards you will see observable positive changes in the child. Perform Emotional Release Therapy any time you know the child has recently experienced physical or emotional pain. If the child has daily contact with others, consider practicing daily release therapy.

Emotional Release with School-Aged Children

School-aged children immediately identify their hurts. They release their hurts into a hand easily and quickly. Afterwards, they are excited by their rewarding experience.

Allison. My twelve-year-old granddaughter, Allison, was left with inch-long red cuts on her chin and forearms after breaking a windowpane with them. While staying with us the following weekend, she agreed to release the initial trauma of the pain and bleeding into my hand. It took her about five minutes. I felt a strong flow of energy enter my hand. Afterwards, she enthusiastically stated, "Grampa, that was neat! It felt great."

An hour later she returned and excitedly exclaimed, "Grampa, my cuts are no longer sore. And look, the incisions have turned from red to white."

Melissa. At that moment my nine-year-old granddaughter, Melissa, spoke up, saying, "Grampa, I have hurts to be healed, too."

I had long been concerned about her because Melissa was a marginal student due to concentration problems. Melissa also interrupted adult conversation and she just could not sit still. She was often hostile and aggressive and had complained to me that she had never had a friend.

For three minutes, with only brief instructions, Melissa released an extremely strong flow of energy into my hand. Afterwards, her face glowed with joy and she said in amazement, "I have never felt this peaceful."

I have no hints as to the nature of her hurts, but those three minutes of releasing emotional hurts changed Melissa's life forever.

When I visited her two weeks later, she jumped into my arms and enthusiastically whispered in my ear, "My first two friends are in the bedroom. I want you to come and meet them."

Later, I asked her mother, "How's Melissa doing?"

She answered, "Melissa has completely changed. Dad, believe it or not, she's now a normal child."

When To Do It

Almost any childhood issue can be alleviated with Emotional Release Therapy. These include expressions of anger, rage, hatred and rebellion, of fear, anxiety, and despair, of depression and grief. Emotional Release Therapy is effective for problems with the family, school, and friends, attention deficits, destructive behavior, allergies, delinquency, the healing of emotional, physical, and interpersonal traumas, and chronic and life-threatening illnesses. Use Emotional Release Therapy with school-age children whenever you think it is appropriate.

Matt, twelve, and Mike, eight, came with their mother for healing. All three suffered from allergies. Experience having taught me that most diseases can be quickly healed by just healing emotional hurts, I practiced Emotional Release Therapy with each of them and they left.

A week later, their mother reported amazing outcomes. Their allergies had disappeared. In addition, hyperactive Matt was now calm and productive, angry and resentful Mike now was loving and cooperative, and their mother had stopped her incessant worrying; she now was calm and relaxed. All three reported being the happiest they had ever been. Such are the pleasant surprises of Emotional Release Therapy.

How to Practice with School-Age Children

School-age children can usually release a lifetime of emotional trauma within ten minutes. They are keenly aware of their emotional hurts. Most visualize well.

Explain how this works. Assure the child that no disclosure of specific circumstances is necessary.

Hand. While sitting, place your dominant hand, flattened straight, on the child's heart.

Color. Ask the child to choose a color to symbolize any hurts.

Unity. Love the child and seek to be one with him or her. Do so until you feel merged with the child.

Pray. Say, "Let us pray," then pray, *God, help _____ release his/her hurt into my hand. I receive it in love and entrust it to your care. Thank you.*

Release. Now tell the child to release his or her hurts into your hand from his or her heart.

Coach. When you feel the heat or energy of the hurt entering your hand, assure the child that he or she is doing it right. Each time the heat release stops, encourage the release of another hurt.

Bless. When the release is finished, with your hand on the child's heart, fill him or her with God's spirit by praying: *"God, use my hand to fill _____ with your love and light, your peace and joy. Thank you. Amen."* Leave your hand there for about a minute.

Experiment with how to use this therapy wisely and well. Tell others how beautifully Emotional Release Therapy transforms children.

12

Becoming Emotionally More Sensitive

Have you ever wanted to become emotionally more sensitive to the needs of others?

Have you ever wanted to be more emotionally involved?

Have you ever wanted to be more caring?

If you feel emotionally closed off from other people, help is on the way here in this chapter. If your heart chakra is closed, you are unable to emotionally respond to others.

The heart is the place in the body where you feel emotions. If your heart has become closed, you have difficulty feeling emotions in yourself or others. With a closed heart, you are a victim. You have been trapped in a situation you could neither understand nor change.

Men are the principal victims of closed hearts. Thinking tends to dominate in men, partly due to male cultural conditioning to think rather than to feel. The ongoing message to boys is that *big* boys do not cry and do not show their feelings. Part of this may be due to the biological effects of the male sex hormone, testosterone.

In addition, for both sexes the hurts of life can be so wounding, or become so unbearably painful, that some must close off their hearts to protect themselves from further hurt. They then escape into their thinking minds as a means of protecting themselves from feeling their hurts.

Advantages of a Closed Heart

Having a closed heart possesses some advantages. A closed heart is not as easily wounded or filled with emotional pain. For this reason, men suffer less from emotion-based diseases such as depression and cancer. Closed hearts make people appear more courageous and capable in times of crisis because men with closed hearts can still think in the midst of crisis while women may become emotionally overwhelmed. Clear thinking, un-hampered by emotional considerations, can be a voca-tional asset in many fields of work. When it lacks sensitivity, however, it can become a destructive liability.

Liabilities of a Closed Heart

In family matters, there are more liabilities than ad-vantages to a closed heart. Closed-hearted people are frustrated in family life because they have trouble ex-pressing their feelings. They have difficulty in emotion-ally giving and receiving love. They often lack a compassionate and nurturing nature. This frustrates and angers wives who do not think their unfeeling husbands deeply care for them.

People with closed hearts still feel emotional pain. But when faced with an acute, chronic, or life-threatening disease, they are less capable of dealing with the emotional struggles involved. They often suffer alone because they have great difficulty in expressing their hurts.

Opening and Closing the Heart

The heart is not closed intentionally. People with closed hearts are incapable of deeply sensing the emotions of others. Emotionally skillful people daily open and close their heart's energy fields many times. The heart center is closed every time one is cautious with other people. In self-defense, the closed heart may still emit the energy of caution, fear, or anger. This is also a handicap, because the closed heart is incapable of picking up the feelings of others, even the positive emotional signals of others that could lead to trust and friendship.

Unless it has been impaired, the heart center naturally opens in situations that are safe, such as when we are with family members and trusted friends.

To Feel, Learn To Open Your Heart

To become an emotionally sensitive person, to be more emotionally involved with loved ones, to be a more caring and nurturing person, learn to open your heart chakra. Emotional Release Therapy offers you a way of changing. With it, you can learn to open your heart to emotionally give and receive love. With it, you can learn how to become a compassionate, sensitive, nurturing person.

Learning to open your heart is a process involving several steps. These steps will take about five hours of your time. Approach this process with curiosity and anticipation. Your life is about to become far more enjoyable and satisfying. Daily family satisfaction and happiness are just around the corner.

1) Remove Your Hurts

First, you must heal your own emotional pain. As long as the emotional hurts are still stored in your emotional energy field, you will be unable to fully feel. Your heart will remain closed to feelings. Now, go back to Chapter 8, Healing Emotional Pain.

Be prepared to spend at least three hours on releasing your hurts and troubling emotional states as described in Chapter 8. Master your ability to release your emotional pain. You will know success when you begin experiencing a deep sense of inner peace and satisfaction.

2) Learn To Control Your Heart

Learn to open and close your heart center as an act of will.

Lie down on your back with your dominant hand over your heart.

To open your heart, choose the image of a flower bud of your choice. The bud represents a closed heart. Place the bud in your heart. Imagine the bud opening up into a blooming flower. This process should open your heart center. Another approach is to imagine opening a window in your heart.

Release. Now release various emotions from your heart into your hand. Note how each of them feels in your hand. In doing this, you are learning to project your feelings toward others. Doing this practice in real-life situations permits others to honestly respond to your emotional interactions with them, permitting richer relationships.

Close your heart by making the flower into a bud again or by closing the window. With a closed heart center, try to transmit emotions from your heart into your hand. You should now feel little or nothing.

Benefits. This practice will help you project your feelings on others so that they can emotionally interact with you. You will better feel the feelings of others so that you can emotionally react to them. And you will gain self-control in your interactions with others. Choose to have an open or closed heart center according to the situation. You will soon be choosing this automatically.

Practice Emoting with Others

These are road tests. Practice your skills of opening your heart to send your feelings to others. You should also be able to open your heart to feel the mood of others and to feel their words and the emotional intent of their actions.

Secretly. You can practice this secretly with friends and loved ones. See if you can project your feelings with your words and actions. See if you can feel the words and actions of others. Cautiously check out your impressions.

In cooperation. Ask a loved one or friend to help you learn. Explain what you have been practicing and why. Interact in a normal way. Frequently share what your heart senses he or she is feeling. Just as often, ask him or her to share impressions of what you are feeling. It is normal for everyone to miss at times.

Bond. Men, emotionally bond with your wife or girlfriend. While lying in bed, have your woman lie on her back. Place your dominant hand on her heart. Open your heart and send various emotions to her through

Health & Healing in the World's Religions

CHRISTIANITY: *"The prayer of faith shall heal the sick, and the Lord shall raise him up."*

HINDUISM: *"Enricher, Healer of disease, be a good friend to us."*

ISLAM: *"The Lord of the worlds created me — and when I am sick, He heals me."*

BUDDHISM: *"To keep the body in good health is a duty — otherwise we shall not be able to keep our mind strong and clear."*

BAHA'I: *"All healing comes from God."*

JUDAISM: *"O Lord, my God, I cried to you for help and you have healed me."*

SIKHISM: *"God is Creator of all, the remover of sickness, the giver of health."*

JAINISM: *"All living beings owe their present state of health to their own Karma."*

ZOROASTRIANISM: *"Love endows the sick body of man with firmness and health."*

TAOISM: *"Pursue a middle course. Thus will you keep a healthy body and a healthy mind."*

Copyright permission courtesy of Marcus Bach

your hand. Try emotions such as love, tenderness, and passion. She will feel these emotions as your hand emits them. When she does, she will no longer doubt your love and commitment to her.

Do not learn all this and then let it slip away with non-use. Your rewards are going to be immense. You are going to be enjoying your own feelings. Your relationships with family and friends are going to be far more rewarding for everyone involved because of their awareness of your emerging compassion or nurturing qualities. You will find yourself far happier and more satisfied than you have ever been.

13

Experiencing God
for the First Time

Have you ever wanted to experience God for the first time?

Have you ever wanted to enter the deepest of spiritual states?

Fifty million Americans have probably never experienced God. This is one of the most closely guarded personal secrets of all time.

Throughout the centuries, saints, mystics, and poets have all referred to the heart as the place where we meet God. The heart is the doorway to God. It is the site where God and our souls can make contact with each other.

So, why is it so difficult to find God? Any time our heart chakra is closed, we cannot experience God. It is like closing and locking a steel door. God cannot get in.

Many men spend lifetimes wondering what the big hoopla about God is all about. They do so because they have never experienced God. They do not talk about it. They think they are some kind of freak. Some respond by putting down God and organized religion. Some respond by indifference toward a God that they have never been able to experience. Most respond by pretending they experience God.

I have known retired men who have spent their entire lives as active church members but have never experienced God. It is their most closely guarded secret. Men who have never experienced God must number in the tens of millions in the United States alone. They do not know why this is true of themselves. But we do. They are victims of closed heart chakras.

Other Reasons for Not Experiencing God

Closed heart chakras are not the only reason people have difficulty experiencing God. Studies show that people who overuse caffeine and nicotine products cannot experience God. This is because these chemicals prevent their brain waves from entering the alpha frequencies where God is experienced. People on a steady diet of rock music also cannot experience God. Rock music which impairs the growth of plants, also impairs the brain's ability to make contact with God. With their steady diet of caffeine-laced beverages and rock music, most church youth report an inability to experience God. Recognizing these factors, many pastors caution their youth against contact with them.

In addition, depressed and grieving people close off their hearts and cannot experience God.

Combining these factors, perhaps half of all Americans are unable to experience God. This realization has given rise to fundamentalist beliefs that focus on rigid rational theological orthodoxy and morality, rather than a first-hand relationship with an unexperienced God. The result is a drop in church attendance among the growing number of people who cannot experience God.

Concentrating on Open Hearts

We cannot do anything to limit the intake of caffeine, nicotine, or rock music. But we can focus upon opening closed heart chakras. You can learn to open your heart to experience God during prayer and during religious rituals.

Begin by undergoing Emotional Release Therapy as described in Chapter 8. Release your painful memories and destructive emotional states.

Then, before praying, place your hand on your heart and open it. Visualize a flower bud in your heart. Then let the flower open into a beautiful bloom. Now your heart should be open. While it is open, pray and do other spiritual disciplines. Note your new experience of God. Experiencing God can include a sense of a oneness with the universe, an awareness of sacredness, an inner peace, love, happiness, and/or satisfaction. It is an unmistakable experience.

Attend a worship service or mass and open your heart in the same way. You will not experience God in all churches. Some churches seemed to be filled with people with closed hearts. But explore various churches until you find one where an open heart brings you God. Pentecostal or Charismatic events are usually filled with the immense power of the Spirit of God.

Once you know how to experience God, you can launch your own spiritual journey. This provides you with another resource for healing yourself.

God and Emotional Release Therapy

If these exercises have not helped you experience God, practicing Emotional Release Therapy on others may prove to be the key. Many people report Emotional Release Therapy to be a spiritual experience. Spiritual bliss sometimes accompanies the practice of Emotional Release Therapy. About twenty percent of the time, I enter into the deepest spiritual state I have ever known. It can last for an hour or two. You must refrain from caffeine and nicotine products for at least an hour before, in order to experience such a state.

Rely on Time-Tested Spiritual Disciplines

Many activities bring us into the presence of God. These time-tested spiritual disciplines work:

Pray daily for the needs of yourself and others.

Seek every opportunity to express love and caring for others freely.

Daily, seek happiness and satisfaction for yourself.

Seek out satisfying friendships.

Actively participate in a religious community that offers you satisfying worship experiences, and prayer and support groups. Both worship and groups can bathe you in a sacred energy that transforms and empowers you with God.

Read sacred or inspired writings.

Part Three:

HEALING YOUR
RELATIONSHIPS

14

Energizing Your Marriage

Can energy exchanges between you and your spouse affect your health?

Can your spouse's energy emissions make you ill?

Are there ways to energize your marriage in order to produce healthy energy?

When the human emotional energy field is filled with painful memories and destructive emotional states, it causes distortions in the physical blueprint energy field. This, in turn, causes many of the diseases in the physical body.

Using Chapters 8 and 10, you should have already used Emotional Release Therapy to restore your emotional energy field to health. But, if you live in a home with your spouse or other loved ones, it may be that your emotional energy field is being constantly endangered by the people with whom you live.

This endangering can even come from those whom you deeply love.

Vana's Story

A Polish physician relates this story. Over a period of years, she had treated nine-year-old Vana for a series of illnesses whose symptoms were clinically puzzling. Fearing for frail Vana's life, she referred Vana to an unusual psychiatrist for evaluation.

This psychiatrist had the clairvoyant ability to see human energy fields and their interactions. She noted that Vana's energy fields were severely depleted. When she invited Vana's mother in to discuss this condition, she observed that the mother was persistently drawing energy from Vana's energy fields, depleting them.

Of course, the mother was innocent of any bad intentions. The psychiatrist taught Vana's mother how to stop being an energy vampire and Vana's health dramatically improved.

In a similar way, your spouse can affect your health.

A depressed spouse becomes an energy vampire who depletes your life energy.

An emotionally distant spouse can also be an energy vampire who unknowingly takes not only your love, but your life energy.

An anxious or angry spouse emits an energy that fills your emotional energy fields with anxiety or anger.

In a marriage where companionship, passion, or commitment are absent, your emotional energy field is bound to become impaired and need ongoing Emotional Release Therapy.

Two Processes for Energizing Your Marriage

During many years as a marriage counselor, I have found that nothing works better at restoring the energy to a marriage than the following two processes. Using these processes is another step on your road back to health. These processes are:

Mutual Emotional Release Therapy
Five minutes of daily prayer together

Guidance for these processes is forthcoming. Remember, this is your healing journey so you must take the lead. Both processes require your spouse's cooperation. You know what to do with the letter on the following page.

Getting Started

These processes can be used at the same time, or you can begin mastering the first process before going on to praying together.

Begin by agreeing on a daily time when you will meet together.

Process One: Emotional Release Therapy

The first process involves using Emotional Release Therapy. Prepare yourself by reading Chapters 6 and 7.

The best way to utilize Emotional Release Therapy is upon each other. This helps you care for each other in a fairly safe, structured setting. Begin by reading Chapter 8 for a thorough understanding of Emotional Release Therapy. Then go to Chapter 10 and use the process on each other as described. The instructions there are complete, so no additional directions need to be added to Emotional Release Therapy here.

My Wife's Emotional Release

I was already a veteran of Emotional Release Therapy when I offered it to my wife. As we lay on our bed, I asked Dana to lie upon her back. I then placed my dominant hand upon her heart.

I have no idea what emotional hurts Dana released during Emotional Release Therapy. It did not matter. These were her private hurts and demons that I respected as her own confidential releases.

But I did know the immense satisfaction of seeing my spouse transformed. As I watched, I saw Dana's face become remarkably peaceful and young, as if the weight of the whole world had been lifted from her shoulders.

Since then, I happily observe that we share the common inner centering and peace that Emotional Release Therapy produces. Our life together is wonderful.

Process Two: Daily Prayer Together

For a couple to pray together daily in the special way I am about to describe produces a truly miraculous improvement in relationship.

Dana and I discovered this prayer process by accident. I had returned home from a prayer workshop with a determination to practice daily prayer with my wife. Dana eagerly embraced my suggestion.

Like millions of couples, our nightly bedtime ritual had been to hug, peck a kiss to the lips, say "Goodnight!" and then turn over to sleep. By simply adding prayer, two surprising but wonderful things happened.

First, we embraced and intended to vocally pray for our needs and for the needs of our loved ones. Then came the first surprise. Dana had been praying aloud for about ten seconds, when we felt heat building up between our bodies. It continued to grow stronger throughout our four-minute prayer.

Afterwards, we discussed it. We agreed that the heat was centered in our energy centers at the throat, heart,

A Letter to your Spouse

Dear Spouse,

Your partner has been courageously fighting for a full return to health. You have been concerned as you watched your spouse battle a chronic or life-threatening medical condition. You may or may not believe in spiritual healing and you may not understand it, but you have observed the actual benefits your spouse is deriving from self-healing efforts.

The next step in the self-healing process requires your help. Not only will this next step help to restore your mate's health, but this process will also benefit you in these ways:

- *It will remove the emotional hurts from throughout your lifetime plus any existing destructive emotional states, bringing you more personal happiness and satisfaction than you have known for some time, through the process of Emotional Release Therapy.*
- *No matter what the present state of your marriage, it will enhance your marriage to the extent that you and your spouse will know lasting peace, cooperation and love through the process of simply praying with your spouse five minutes a day.*

Are you willing to follow through with these two processes with your spouse?

If so, tell your spouse that you are willing to actively take part in the next steps needed to help him or her get well and lead a full life.

Thank you for reading this letter.

Walter L. Weston

diaphragm, abdomen, and groin areas. Somehow our energy centers were stimulating each other. We speculated that somehow our energy centers were merging. Unknown to us then, this process was not only uniting but also harmonizing our energy fields.

The next morning we experienced the second surprise. The quality and depth of our relationship dramatically improved. The rough edges disappeared as bickering, irritations, and blaming ended. Intimacy levels deepened with the quality and quantity of personal sharing improving to joyous levels.

As the days passed and we continued our nightly prayers, we discovered ourselves resolving our disagreements more easily. Our love, passion, companionship, and commitment reached new heights.

We have continued our nightly prayers for a dozen years. Now we experience only a minor amount of heat and energy between us that continues to unite and harmonize our energy fields.

Dana and I had undergone marriage counseling several times. We have been deeply involved in leading marriage enrichment and communications labs. I have counseled hundreds of troubled marriages. We now realize that the results of daily praying, while embracing, far surpasses all those approaches and their outcomes.

We do not expect most other couples to experience such strong heat between their bodies nor to have such early dramatic results. Yet the reports from dozens of couples who have used this approach duplicate our results. When you then add Emotional Release Therapy to the formula for happy marriages, the results are truly spectacular.

While at a St. Louis conference, I met David and Gloria, who intended to file for divorce when they returned home to Denver. They spoke sadly of irreconcilable differences. I gave them printed directions for praying together. A month later, David phoned to report that they daily prayed together and were now gloriously happy.

Directions for Praying Together

These directions for praying together are so simple that you may think nothing special can possibly happen.

Lie down and embrace face to face. (This sounds like a strange position in which to pray but it is the only way that your energy centers can touch.)

Pray aloud for the needs of loved ones and yourselves. (Your prayers should not be vague or wishy-washy blessings. They should intentionally state needed results, just like healing prayers. Below are prayer models that you might wish to use until you develop your own confident style.)

Agree to vocally pray together daily for two whole weeks before you evaluate the results.

Remember, praying together produces healthy human energy fields, creates a bonding of unity, and facilitates understanding, reconciliation, healing, and growth in relationships.

Prayer Models for Couples Praying Together

Each prayer can be said by one spouse or as pray-along. In pray-along, one person speaks a phrase and then both people say the prayer together. The three ellipses between words mark the pray-along phrases.

Couple: 1. *God...we thank you for this day. We pray for our family, for [name them]_____. Fill them with your love and light . . . provide for their needs...and protect them from all harm. We pray for _____. Heal them and make them whole . . . in body, mind and spirit.*

We pray for ourselves, God. We place our concerns in your hands. Provide for our needs . . . and unite us as one as we share life together. Grant us your peace . . . and refresh us while we sleep. Guide and sustain us . . . in all that is before us. Thank you. Amen.

Couple: 2. *God, we thank you for this day . . . with all its work . . . joys and challenges. We praise you for being with us . . . offering us the gift of life. Grant us your peace . . . as we end this day . . . and offer us wholeness in body, mind and spirit.*

Deepen our unity with each other . . . and with you. We pray for the following concerns: _____. Be with us, God . . . as we sleep . . . protecting and nurturing us . . . and restoring us into the image of your perfect creation. Amen.

Deepening love. *God, thank you . . . for joining us together . . . in the rich bond of marriage. We remember . . . the faith, hope and love . . . of our wedding day. We rejoice . . . in our struggles and celebrations.*

We keep before us the sacred wisdom: "Love is patient and kind. Love is not rude. Love does not . . . insist on its own way. It is not irritable nor resentful. Love rejoices in the right. Love bears all things . . . believes all things . . . hopes all things . . . endures all things."

God, fill our souls . . . with your love . . . that we might always . . . cherish and honor each other . . . in gracious love. Amen.

Grandparents 1. *God, we thank you . . . for all the blessings of this day. We thank you for our children, [name them] ____, and their families. Fill them with your love and light . . . provide for their needs . . . and protect them from all harm.*

We pray especially for _____. Bring healing and wholeness to them . . . in body, mind, and spirit.

We pray for ourselves. Provide us with meaning and challenge each day. We entrust ourselves to your care. Grant us wholeness and renewal as we sleep. Thank you. Amen.

Grandparents 2. *God, we thank you . . . for the richness of the years. We treasure the memories of earlier days . . . with our children as they were growing up.*

We thank you for the joys of sharing continuing love . . . with our children, their spouses, and our grandchildren. Bless our children and their families . . . and hold them in your care.

We pray for our own needs. Continue to bless us with health, happiness and financial resources. We continue to rely upon your sustaining love and guidance. Grant us your peace and renew us as we sleep. Thank you. Amen.

15

Energizing Your Household

Can the energy exchanges between you and others with whom you live affect your health?

Can a child's energy emissions make you ill?

Are there ways to energize your home in order to fill it with healthy energy?

Thirty-year-old Valerie still lived at home with her mother. She came to me for counseling about her eating disorder. She also expressed an immense rage toward her mother, Beverly.

Knowing that Valerie's problems were far beyond my professional competence, I tried, without success, to refer her to a psychiatrist. Before departing from her life, I gave her an extensive warning about the consequences of her cruel behavior toward her mother.

I stated, "Valerie, if you do not stop badgering your mother, she is going to get sick and die. Please find the professional help you so badly need."

Two years later, Valerie phoned me, and in a desperate voice, said, "Dr. Weston, my mother is dying of cancer. She only has a few days to live. Will you do healing with her at the hospital?"

I replied, "Ask your mother if she wants to see me. If so, I will come. But I think she will refuse because she wants to die."

Beverly refused to see me and a few days later died.

The Stress of Raising Children

Being a parent is stressful. Adding to this stress are extra burdens placed upon families of children with birth defects, with chronic and life-threatening illnesses, with alcohol and drug abuse problems, with learning disabilities, with behavioral problems; upon single parents and step-parents; upon families in poverty, in a violent or criminal environment.

Additional stress is on children who are being or have been physically, emotionally, or sexually abused or who have lived through painful emotional and physical traumas.

How many of the children and parents in these situations also suffer acute, chronic, or life-threatening illnesses because of the stress these problems place upon the whole household? Or the build-up of painful memories?

Preventive Medicine

The greatest preventive medicine in the world is an environment in your home in which you can find happiness and satisfaction.

If you suffer from a chronic or life-threatening illness, you will find inner peace with Emotional Release Therapy. You can also help other household members release their hurts.

But these will only temporarily heal your medical condition if you live in a hostile or unhappy household environment. The negative energy emitted by unhappy people is just as lethal to you as the energy of your own painful memories and destructive emotional states have been.

When you live in a strenuous environment, you cannot prevent yourself from being drawn into the deadly interpersonal interactions involved. These have the power to once again distort your energy fields and make you sick.

Household Preventive Medicine Options

So how do you create an environment in your home in which you can find happiness and satisfaction?

You can leave your household, divorcing yourself from those who cause you pain.

You can find an alternative place for the pain-causers in your household to live.

You can seek out the help of a professional family therapist.

You can fill your home with a sacred energy that energizes everyone into being loving, peaceful, cooperative, responsible persons.

Let us look at the last option. It works. It is free. It energizes everyone in your household.

Filling Your Home with Sacred Energy

When our children were growing up, we made several efforts to pray daily together. But we always eventually dropped our prayer efforts because we found them to be a boring and meaningless activity. Almost too late, we made a wonderful discovery about prayer. Prayer is not boring; it is the way that we pray together that produces boredom.

Our discovery involved having everyone share their personal needs and then praying for God to bless those personal needs. This practice expressed our loving concern for every household member. In this way each of us felt valued and supported. It also expressed the unique individuality of each person.

But the greatest payoff came later. God actually began blessing us. We experienced God's presence guiding and sustaining us.

Our prayers also created a sacred energy that permeated our home. We could feel God's love and peace in every room in the house. But it was more than just a feeling. We were being constantly bathed in God's energy. This was changing us. His love and peace truly filled us and made us loving and peaceful.

Yes, God began transforming us into his image. We were becoming more sacred. And thus more loving, caring, peaceful, cooperative, and responsible to ourselves and with each other. We all changed for the better. We each found the happiness and satisfaction for which we so deeply yearned.

If you energize your home with God, you will attain these same results. It takes a few minutes a day of time and effort. It means developing new skills. It means persuading everyone to give it a try.

It is also another step in your journey back to health. Such a prayer practice will help your energy fields become even healthier, but will also energize them for your maximum recovery. In addition, it will do so for every member of your household.

How about it? Do you want to fill your home with sacred energy and energize each of your loved ones with God? If so, here is a letter that you might wish to share with everyone in your household:

A Letter to Your Household

Dear Household Member,

Your loved one has been courageously fighting for a full return to health. You have been concerned as you watched him/her battle a chronic or life-threatening medical condition.

You may or may not understand what he/she is doing, but you have observed the actual benefits deriving from his/her self-healing efforts.

The next step in the self-healing process requires your help. If you do not cooperate, you are contributing negative energy. The negative energy in your home is literally killing him/her. You can help change all of this.

This next step asks for you to meet ten minutes a day for prayer with everyone in your household.

If you are willing to do so, tell your loved one that you are willing to actively take part in the next step needed to help him/her to get well and lead a full life.

Thank you for acting to save his/her life.

Walter Weston

Plans for Beginning Praying Together

Show each person the above letter.

Hear their agreement to join you in daily prayer. Proceed with those who agree.

Ask for a two-week commitment to daily prayer, after which you will all sit down and evaluate the personal results. Then, vote about continuing.

Agree upon a regular daily time for praying together. The best times are after a meal, in early evening, or in late evening.

As the leader, keep everyone informed. If anyone misses a prayer time, tell him you missed him and expect to see him at the next prayer time. If someone displays indifference, ignore it. All will eventually come around.

You lead the earliest prayer times, but later ask anyone who seems ready to take a turn.

Ask everyone to hold hands before beginning the prayer.

Plans for Prayer Sessions

Healing prayers focus upon the specific needs of a person. This personal approach brings a power to prayer that general blessings do not. The person feels valued, understood, supported, and loved as a special and unique individual. Under these circumstances, he or she also experiences God more powerfully. The sacred outcome is that God actually offers an energy that heals the person.

In a like manner, your prayers together focusing on specific concerns and needs of each person in the group has the same powerful effect.

How can you come to know the specific needs of each person?

The best way is to ask each person to express a need before the prayer. It may be best to write it down so the pray-er gets it straight. You begin by explaining that you want everyone to express a specific need so those needs can be used in your prayer. You might express your own need first.

How do you pray for those needs without anyone feeling embarrassed or manipulated?

Do not manipulate, preach, or advise during prayer.

Do bless people with support and a helpful outcome.

Express your prayer requests for others in the same way in which you would want it offered to you.

Respect the spiritual freedom and dignity of everyone, even children.

Never, ever, offer a joke or pun during prayer. People tend to take prayer words literally. (I confess that my wife and I do joke and pun, however, knowing each other well after some 4,000 prayers together.)

How do you learn to pray in this manner?

Begin with the prayer models provided below. Eventually, find your own style.

Prayer Models

Prayer from knowing. You already know many of the concerns which face members of your household. Just include each of them in your prayer. Here is an example:

> God, thank you for gathering us together as loved ones. We seek your love and power for our lives. Fill our home with your love and peace.
>
> God, bless us tomorrow as we go about our separate tasks. Provide for each of our needs and protect us from all harm. Inspire us to live life fully and joyously. We pray for each other's needs.

Bless Fran in school tomorrow. Help her to remember what she needs to know and to find the friends she needs.

Help Bill find the job that he so badly needs. Let an opportunity just come to him.

Dad's back is hurting him. Heal his back and take away the pain. Thank you.

God, I am concerned about work. Help things flow smoothly for me tomorrow.

We thank you for the food we are about to eat. May it nourish our bodies.

Thank you for hearing our prayer. Amen.

Prayer from group sharing their needs. After seeking prayer requests from everyone, pray for those requests.

God, we are thankful to be here together. We come to you as a means of supporting each other and of seeking your help for our lives.

It is so much easier when we can share our needs and receive help from you and our loved ones. Having shared our needs, we now bring them to you.

John has expressed his need to be understood. God, we pray that you will help each of us understand John better.

Amy is struggling with her math. God, we pray that you will grant her your peace and help her to improve her understanding and performance in math.

Dad needs more help in the yard. God, help us all to take more responsibility for the yard.

God, I want more hugs from everyone here. Let them surround me with love.

God, bless us as a family. Bathe us in your love and peace. Fill our home with your presence. Provide for our needs and protect us from all harm. Thank you. Amen.

Dinner Table Grace.

God, the giver and sustainer of all life, remove our tiredness and fill us with life anew. We thank you for this food and those who have prepared it. Surround us with your presence and make us one with all whom we love. May your joy fill our hearts as we enjoy the remainder of this day. Amen.

Table Grace with Children.

God, thank you for making each of us special and important. Fill us with your love and help us to love and care for each other. Provide for our needs. May your peace fill our hearts and make us strong. We thank you for this food. May it nourish our bodies. Amen.

16

Family Rituals of Affirmation

Persons of all ages need to hear words from loved ones who accept, affirm, support, and appreciate them. If these are not forthcoming within the family, people can spend a lifetime feeling inadequate, unloved, unhappy, and angry. When you are fighting for your health, words of affirmation are a welcome means for boosting your morale and self-confidence.

If you are now daily praying with your spouse, family, or household members, invite them to join you in these affirmations. If you are not, they may still go along with these affirmations.

Be seated around a table, in chairs or on the floor in some approximation of a circle. The same person can lead each session or each family member can take a turn at leadership. Even toddlers can take part to receive affirmation.

There are four rituals of affirmation. You can do these as often as you choose, weekly or monthly. All should begin with the **Opening Unison Family Affirmation Prayer** and end with the **Closing Affirming Prayer**.

First Family Ritual of Affirmation

Begin with Opening Unison Family Affirmation Prayer

God, we have gathered as a family to affirm one another. We forgive each other for any pain we have experienced and ask the forgiveness of any family member we have hurt.

We promise to accept and to respect each other. We affirm our love and support for each other. We are thankful to be family. Amen.

1) AFFIRMING STRUGGLES. Each person states where he or she is struggling in life, with all family members offering an affirmation.

Examples: *"Boredom at school," "being lonely and having no friends," "my medical condition," "the pimples on my face which make me look ugly," "my failure to make the team," "my inability to run like other people," "stress on the job," and "my anger toward ____."* Here is the ritual:

a) **Statement of Personal Struggles.** A person says: *"I am struggling with ____."*

b) **The Ritual of Affirmation.** The family in unison responds: *"____, we unconditionally love and support you, just as you are, in all of your sacred preciousness."*

Closing Affirming Prayer.

God, we thank you for this time together. May your love fill our whole family with joy and peace. Bring healing and wholeness to each of us individually and to all of us as a family. Amen.

Second Family Ritual of Affirmation

Begin with **Opening Unison Family Affirmation Prayer.**

God, we have gathered as a family to affirm one another. We forgive each other for any pain we have experienced and ask the forgiveness of any family member we have hurt.

We promise to accept and to respect each other. We affirm our love and support for each other. We are thankful to be family. Amen.

2) AFFIRMING PERSONAL FOCUS. Each person states his or her present major life focus, with all family members offering affirmation.

Examples of focuses: *"Get a 'B' in my science class," "I want to be well again." "deepen my relationship with* _____," *"save enough money to* _____" *"overcome my fear of failure," "learn patience and control my temper."* Here is the ritual:

a) **Statement of Personal Focus.** A person says: *"The present major focus of my life is to* _____."

b) **The Ritual of Affirmation.** Family in unison responds: "_____, *we unconditionally love and support you in your focus."*

Closing Affirming Prayer.

God, we thank you for this time together. May your love fill our whole family with joy and peace. Bring healing and wholeness to each of us individually and to all of us as a family. Amen.

Third Family Ritual of Affirmation

Begin with the **Opening Unison Family Affirmation Prayer:**

God, we have gathered as a family to affirm one another. We forgive each other for any pain we have experienced and ask the forgiveness of any family member we have hurt.

We promise to accept and to respect each other. We affirm our love and support for each other. We are thankful to be family. Amen.

3) AFFIRMING UNIQUE TRAITS. Each family member is affirmed by all others as each individually addresses the person by name and states a quality they value in him.

Examples of qualities: *"Your gentle smile," "your sense of humor," "the way you worked to achieve _____," "the way you handled _____," and "your understanding when I _____."* Here is the ritual:

a) **The Ritual of Affirmation.** Go around the circle, focusing on one person at a time so that each family member can individually offer affirmation. Address the person by name and say: "_____, a *valued quality I see in you and appreciate is* _____."

Closing Affirming Prayer.

God, we thank you for this time together. May your love fill our whole family with joy and peace. Bring healing and wholeness to each of us individually and to all of us as a family. Strengthen us in our struggles, guide us in our focuses, and strengthen those

*qualities in us which are blessings to others. May only
good come to us and flow through us. Bless us that we
might be blessings to each other. Thank you. Amen.*

Fourth Family Ritual of Affirmation

The purpose of this family ritual is to help a family
member work through a hurt from the past or present.
It can be a hurt, a failure, a disappointment, a betrayal,
a confession or a mistake. It can be initiated by any family
member. Gather in a circle. The speaker tells his or her
story from a personal viewpoint, including feelings experienced at the time of the event.

Example: *"I went to physical education class today.
We were playing basketball. The teacher told me I was
too awkward to play. He told me to sit and watch. I was
crushed and embarrassed. I felt I was treated unfairly. I
do not want to go back there ever again."*

One listener needs to take the responsibility of patiently
drawing out the teller's story, including emotions. Should
the teller not mention feelings, the active listener can gently
intervene with questions like, *"What were you feeling at
that moment?"* or *"What are you feeling right now?"*

The power to heal is present in the total uncondi-
tional acceptance of the teller's pain by loving people.
As you listen, realize that this is the teller's story, the
teller's truth. It is the teller's perception, interpretation,
and response.

Do *not* correct, argue with, object to, moralize, blame,
criticize, warn, threaten, advise, be impatient, lecture, or
instruct the teller. The teller will discover for himself all
the truths you would like to offer.

Give the teller your full attention. If the teller becomes emotional, do not touch or intervene with words. Any such intervention eases the impact of necessary pain, demeans the teller, and short-circuits the potential for healing.

Opening Affirmative Prayer.

> *God, we have gathered here to offer support to _____. We accept and respect the depth of his/her hurt. We affirm the sacred worth of ____. We promise to listen compassionately and to respond in love and affirmation. Thank you. Amen.*

a) **The Story as Told by the Teller.** An active listener helps to draw out the story and to focus upon the expression of the feelings involved.

b) **Group Ritual of Affirmation.** After the story is completed, the group addresses the teller by name and states: "_____, *we unconditionally love and support you in your hurt.*"

Closing Prayer.

> "*God, heal the hurt. Restore newness of life to ____. Make him/her whole in body, mind and spirit. Thank you. Amen.*

PART FOUR:

HEALING YOUR BODY

17

The Basics of Physical Healing

Spiritual healing is the most widely used form of healing in the world. It is used in most religions and cultures. Spiritual healing uses prayer and touch to achieve healing outcomes. If you have ever prayed, you already have a head start in what you need to know. Your competence in practicing physical healing increases:

- *when a scientific understanding is added to your existing beliefs. At this time, it might be helpful to review Chapter 5, Scientific Foundations.*
- *as you gain knowledge about healing gathered from the experience of healers in the United States and many other nations.*

Value Your Prayers

Prayer is the primary means by which all humanity makes contact with God. Your prayers release God's healing power into your body, power which scientists have measured as an energy emitted at the frequency of plus or minus 7.83 hertz. As you will discover, your own diminished physical vitality or energy does not reduce the healing power of your prayers.

Prayer increases the healing energy within your body, but the touch of your own hands during prayer increases the amount of energy entering your body.

Inner qualities increasing the healing power of your prayers include:

> The emotional healing of your painful memories and hurts and of your destructive emotional states. When you have been emotionally healed, it requires little effort for physical healing to follow.
> Your desire to become well.
> Your confidence, faith, trust, and assurance that God wants you to become well.
> Your inner experience of God's presence, love, joy, and peace.
> Your ability to flow with God.
> Your persistence in bathing your body in healing energy.
> The intentions of your prayers to heal yourself. Prayer models will be offered for your use.

The more qualities you can maximize, the more likely you are to be physically healed. Trust the process of prayer. Trust that through your prayers, you are bringing God's healing power into your life.

Value Your Hands

The energy emitted by your hands express your heart's intentions. The touch of your dominant hand upon your heart can fill you with the energy of faith and hope, of love and nurturing, of comfort and peace, of healing and new life.

God works inevitably through human hands to fill us with his power and other sacred qualities. When your intention is to heal, your dominant hand emits a sacred energy that heals. When your intention is to release the hurt from your heart, your hand receives the hurt. When your intention is to fill your heart with love and peace, your hand will emit sacred love and peace into your heart and your whole being.

Your own personal experiences will convince you of the truth of these statements. Value the abilities and power of your hands.

Value Charged Healing Materials

Scientists have known for forty years that the healing energy emitted by your hands can be imparted to cotton and wool cloth, water, and surgical gauze. These materials will have the same healing effect as your hands.

This assertion does not sound very spiritual, but think about it. Sacred waters and the garments of saints have been reputed to have healing effects throughout the centuries. You are just intentionally creating the same thing.

A cotton dish towel can be charged with healing energy by rolling it up and holding it between your hands. Offer a prayer asking God to use your hands to charge the towel. Charge the towel for fifteen to thirty minutes. After the initial prayer, your hands know what to do and how to do it, so you can watch television, read, or talk.

Then place the towel on your bare skin wherever it is most needed, for eight to twenty-four hours a day. You know it is charged when you place it against your bare skin for several minutes because you can feel a slight heat or energy being emitted by it. A healing towel holds its charge for weeks. It acts as an intravenous tube in constantly dripping healing energy into your energy fields.

Charged towels can be used for trauma injuries, back pain, arthritis, skin conditions, heart disease, headaches, and any localized disease.

*Healing charged cotton towels provide an
ongoing release of healing energy to you.*

Containers of water are charged with healing energy in the same way. Glass containers are preferable to plastic, but both work. You can charge up to a gallon at a time by holding the container between your hands for fifteen to thirty minutes. Offer a prayer asking God to use your hands to charge the water. Drink the water, about two ounces at a time, with meals and at bedtime. It flows into every cell of the body.

I have observed charged healing water heal about every disease imaginable. Just remember to take it seriously. Honor it. Cherish it. Use it regularly and with the expectation that healing will result.

You can give your healing tool a pet name. One of my clients with a brain tumor called the jug I charged for him Walt Water.

An Overview of Physical Healing

This overview clarifies the steps we will be covering that will guide you into self-healing.

Daily and more. Practice healing daily. Try one daily half-hour session followed by two other five- or ten-minute sessions.

An experiment. View it as an experiment. Yes, this is serious business, but be curious. Be aware of its emotional, spiritual, and physical effects upon you. I can promise you that you will feel more peaceful and serene.

Emotional healing first. Always practice emotional healing before going on to physical healing. Emotional hurts and fixated destructive emotional states sabotage all physical healing efforts.

Tissue shock second. If you have trauma injuries or tissue that may be shocked by the effects of your disease, then first remove the pain and shock existing in diseased tissue before proceeding to physical healing. All body tissue is emotionally conscious of the pain inflicted upon it. The presence of this tissue pain inhibits physical healing.

Open energy fields. Always open your energy fields to receive the healing energy you are about to impart to it. Your energy fields may be protecting themselves from outside energies, including your own healing hands or towels.

Hand placement. Use both hands. If your disease is localized, place your dominant hand there with your other hand near it. My favorite technique is to place my dominant hand on my heart and the other hand on my diaphragm. Remember, no matter where you touch, the healing energy transforms your whole energy field to a white energy that is about twice the normal size of your energy field.

A sacred act. Let your healing efforts be practiced in a sacred way. The prayers you use will set your sacred mood.

Measuring the effects. How do you know if you are being helped? First, you will feel a sense of inner peace and well-being. This will be followed by more optimism. You will find your physical vitality increasing. Do not squander this renewed vitality by increasing your physical activity. The increasing feeling of vitality is due to the healing energy working within you to heal your disease. Do not use it to do extra work or play. Conserve your energy so it can be used for its intended purpose, healing. Only you and your doctor can assess any long-term improvement in your medical condition. Trust the process you have begun.

Can I Learn To Heal Myself?

If you can learn to follow a cooking recipe, or to tend a garden, or to paint a room, you can learn to heal yourself. Physical healing is easy, far easier than emotional healing, and that is the problem. It is so easy that you may not think you are doing anything so powerful as physical healing.

The closest comparison would be to taking an antibiotic. You swallow the antibiotic and physically feel nothing, but the antibiotic is quietly healing your infection.

During spiritual healing, you may physically feel little or nothing, though emotionally and spiritually you do sense changes in yourself. With both, you eventually get well. So, yes, you can heal yourself, if you do not quit out of boredom or doubt.

Would You Like Others To Assist You?

With medical treatment, Rose's doctor gave her one chance in a hundred to survive an inoperable cancer that had spread throughout her abdomen.

I taught Rose self-healing techniques and suggested she enlist the healing help of her three grown daughters. Her daughters were excited by the invitation and responded well when I led them in a healing session with Rose in her home.

Two or three evenings a week, they practiced spiritual healing with Rose. Meanwhile, Rose underwent a monthly chemotherapy treatment. Six months later, Rose was cancer-free.

I have witnessed similar healing success stories involving the help of spouses, sisters, and friends.

In self-healing, you are in charge. Part of your self-healing may come from sources other than yourself. You have the option of inviting others to help with their prayers and touch. You have the option of going to where others offer you healing. Such options will be detailed in the coming chapters.

18

Complete Physical Healing

You are the only one who is responsible for your ongoing healing efforts. Do not expect others to share your degree of enthusiasm. You are in charge of your own healing efforts. Gain the cooperation of those who are willing, but do not waste your energy trying to convince those who will not cooperate or support your efforts. This is your journey. Respect and enjoy it.

Practicing Healing Skills

Practice transmitting energy. With fingers straight, place the palms and fingers of both hands against each other. Then pull them apart about half an inch. Try to send energy through each hand to the other. Every person can be taught to transmit energy in this way. Sense the energy between your hands. Now, while continuing to sense this energy, slowly bring your hands apart, until you can no longer feel it. Then move your hands together until they touch.

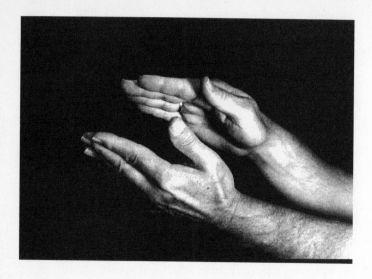

*Everyone can learn to emit energy with their hands,
but it must be attuned by caring and intention.*

An additional experiment is to cup your hands together as if you are holding an orange. Then move your
hands rapidly in opposite circular motions. You will
sense an energy build-up. When we care and we pray,
this energy is transformed into God's healing energy. By
touching yourself during prayer, you transmit the healing energy to your own body.

Your own healing hands. Before each prayer, quiet
yourself and concentrate on being one with God. Use your
hands for transmitting healing energy during each prayer.
To heal a physical condition, if possible place your dominant hand on the area needing healing, with the other hand
on the opposite side. Or place your dominant hand over
your heart and the other hand over your diaphragm.

Leave your hands in place for fifteen minutes following a prayer so the energy can continue to flow. Remain in a state of prayer during this time.

Halting the flow. After any healing effort, stop the flow of the healing energy emitting from your hands by rubbing the palms briskly against each other, or rinsing them with water, or dipping them in saltwater. If you forget this step, you may experience an energy drain.

Self-Healing First Aid

You can practice self-healing as first aid in daily living. This provides opportunities for experimenting and practicing prayer touch-healing. It can also be done calmly, in contrast to the urgency of healing a major medical condition. Torn muscles, bruises, broken bones, damaged cartilage, cuts, burns, and sunburn all respond to self-healing touch prayer. This is healing first aid.

The faster you begin healing treatment, the quicker the response. Begin it within ten minutes of receiving the injury and you may be symptom-free within minutes or hours. If you wait twenty-four hours, the results diminish. You can practice healing at the same time you are applying ice, lotion, or aloe vera to the afflicted area.

Removing Emotional and Tissue Trauma

Emotional Shock. After any physical trauma, practice Emotional Release Therapy upon yourself, releasing the emotional shock of the injury from your heart. This takes only a minute.

Tissue Trauma. Remove the trauma in physical tissue by placing your dominant hand over the damaged area. Pray, *God, help my tissue release its shock into my hand.*

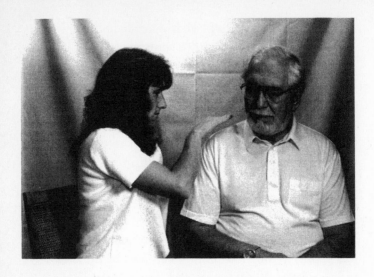

*You can slightly but definitely feel
the trauma energy entering your hand*

Thank you. Amen. Mentally pull the hurt out of the tissue while silently or verbally apologizing to the tissue for its hurt. This takes one to two minutes.

Touch-Healing. Place your healing (dominant) hand on the trauma area. Pray, *God, heal this wound. Thank you. Amen.* Hold your hand there for about five minutes.

Outcome. This produces a dramatic improvement in healing rate beyond that of touch alone.

A trauma injury case. An eighty-year-old physician, Dr. Hubert Hensel, survived a plane crash. He broke his right arm, sternum, and eye socket and cracked seven ribs, and he required seven hours of reconstructive surgery on his face. Following the facial surgery, Dr. Hensel immediately began touch self-healing. Within a week his face had healed without a scar and his broken bones healed within four weeks.

A cut. You can heal a cut on the finger by removing the emotional trauma of the injury from your heart, drawing the trauma pain from the tissue at the wound site, and placing the fingers of either hand around the finger for fifteen minutes. If this is done within minutes of receiving the cut, it may be healed without a scar within forty-eight hours. There will be no pain or discomfort. Be one with God while focusing your intentions on transmitting healing energy.

For sunburn, remove the tissue trauma from your sunburned skin. Then touch each sunburned area for about one minute with your transmitting hand. Place your other hand over your heart area. To be most effective, this procedure must be applied within the first twelve hours of sunburn or even before. By the following day, the skin damage has been completed and your efforts will meet with more difficulty.

After any healing prayer, continue to concentrate on experiencing a oneness with God and the area being healed. Alternate this with the intention of transmitting healing energy, imagining the desired effects. Once you become experienced in performing these two processes, you will learn to continue the healing flow while involved in other activities, such as conversation, reading, or watching television. You will sense when you are able to do this.

Self-healing of Chronic Conditions

Arthritis is a good model for healing a chronic condition. Initially, work on only the worst arthritic joint, such as a knee. Remove trauma from the tissue with your hands. Then, place your hands for ten minutes on either side and then reverse hand positions for another ten minutes. Do this once daily for five consecutive days. You will then notice the beneficial effects and can begin working on other arthritic joints.

Note again that this is a process that works somewhat as an antibiotic, as the effects build up over a period of time. Apply the same procedure for hearing and sight losses, skin diseases, heart damage, cancers, and other diseases.

Two Hands Are Better Than One

In practicing touch-healing prayer, invite another person to place his/her dominant hand over yours as often as possible. The healing flow and the results will be boosted fourfold.

Self-Healing of Your Medical Condition

This self-healing exercise is suitable for healing an acute, chronic, or life-threatening condition. Before beginning, place your hands on the affected area. If you do not know where you need to be healed, place your dominant hand on your heart and the other on your diaphragm.

1) A Prayer for Your Self-Healing

God, I need your help. I ask you to begin healing me, even as I pray. May your healing power flow through my hands and spread throughout my body, healing whatever needs to be healed.

God, be with me as I now practice Emotional Release Therapy on myself by choosing a color to represent my emotional pain and stress. I now release that color, a symbol of all my emotional pain, into my dominant hand on my heart.

(Take all the time you need to do this, for your hurts may be contributing to your medical condition. Afterwards, leave your dominant hand on your heart and continue praying.)

God, let your love and peace flow from my hand into my heart, filling me with your presence. Thank you.

God, I choose to become well. Let your creative, renewing power flow through my hands, renewing all my energy fields, that they might reflect the perfect health you intend for me. And let your sacred life course through my body, renewing every cell and organ, making me well. Heal me in body, mind, and spirit and grant me your peace. Thank you for the renewal that is flowing through me.

God, I know you want me to be well. I entrust my life to your care. Thank you. Amen.

Now imagine God's presence as a pure white healing light flowing from your dominant hand. Say the following prayer as you seek to merge and become one with God:

God, I ask you to come into my life and merge with me. Enable me to be one with you as we unite in Spirit. Let your healing white light flow from my hand throughout my whole body. I sense your presence and light pervading my whole being. I accept this healing. I accept your peace. I ask that wherever your light and love touch, I become whole. Let my healing continue. Amen.

2) Your Own Three-a-Day Prayer Sessions

Place one or both hands on either side of the area needing to be healed. Or place your dominant hand on your heart and the other on your diaphragm. Do so for ten minutes at a time, morning, afternoon, and evening as you pray:

God, use my hands as channels for your healing love, so that wherever I place my hands, your healing flow enters and heals me. May this healing begin now and continue until I am well. Thank you. Amen.

3) Use Healing-Charged Materials

Find or request a cotton towel or a pitcher of water. Hold either between your hands for fifteen minutes, charging them with healing energy. Pray:

God, use my hands to place your healing power in this towel (or water). Let it provide a steady supply of healing energy for my whole body. Thank you. Amen.

Place the towel over your lungs and heart. If you are healing a trauma injury, place the towel on the trauma area. Take a sip of the water hourly.

4) A Daily Healing Prayer by a Loved One

When you ask a loved one to pray with you, he or she may appear to be reluctant. This reluctance has nothing to do with not wanting to pray with you. It is just that most persons have never prayed aloud with someone. They feel awkward in doing something new. You might approach loved ones in this way: "I want to be soaked in prayer as I cope with this illness. I believe prayer will add to my healing. Would you pray with me? While doing so, can we join hands?"

Then provide the following healing prayer. Note that he or she may know how to pray without this prayer, but ask him or her to use this particular prayer because its focus is upon healing.

Ask your loved one to pray with you daily. If he or she lives with or near you, request three prayer sessions a day. Remember to be touched during each prayer, on the area needing to be healed or by holding hands.

Consider practicing Emotional Release Therapy prior to each prayer session.

Then ask your loved ones to pray:

> *God, thank you for _____. Thank you for his or her birth and life, hopes and dreams, and for our life together.*
>
> *God, you are the creator and sustainer of all life. With you, all things are possible. Use me as your channel for healing. May your healing power flow through my heart and hands and into _____.*
>
> *Now, heal _____ in body, mind, and spirit. Recreate and renew every cell and organ of her/his body. Unite us with God, making us one in spirit. Thank you for the healing that is taking place. Amen."*

Keep your hands on your loved one and begin the following healing process:

A. Seek to form a spiritual oneness with your loved one. Silently pray:

> *God, make me one with _____ in body, mind, and spirit. Bless this unity that it might produce wholeness. This is the healing trinity of God, you, and the healee.*

B. Become aware of your hands. Seek to transmit a healing energy with your hands while silently praying:

135

God, use my hands to transmit your healing power.

C. Mentally visualize the intended results, silently praying:

God, enable ____ to be restored into his/her perfect genetic image.

D. Visualize twin objects and merge them into one, with one object representing you and the other your loved one.

With hands still in place, talk with your loved one in a conversational manner. The two most intimate and spiritual human interchanges are touch and speech. They help the attunement and utilization of the healing energy.

Concluding spoken prayer:

"God, fill _____ with your presence. Let this healing begin now and continue throughout the coming hours and days. Thank you for the healing that is now taking place. Amen."

5) Requesting Absent Prayer

At the onset of illness, have someone request prayer from family, friends, strangers, churches, prayer groups and prayer chains. Distribute copies of An Absent Prayer for Healing to loved ones. Clearly tell loved ones, "I am counting on you to pray for me every day. I need the energy of your prayers to help me get well."

Directions for Absent Prayer

God does nothing except through prayer. Prayer is the medium for God's miracles of healing. Tell others of your concern as you provide them with copies of this prayer. When two or more are together, pray aloud together. If you have only one copy of the prayer, do *"pray-along,"* saying a phrase and having the others repeat it after you.

6) An Absent Prayer for Healing

God, thank you for _____. I am worried about her/him and am now praying for his/her recovery. Heal _____ in body, mind and spirit and grant her/him your peace. Thank you. Amen.

Now, sense God and visualize the person or the name and then, in your mind, unite God, the person, and yourself into one—a merging of the three of you. Pray again, saying:

God, join us together in oneness with you. Amen.

Hold that sense of merged oneness in your mind. Now, deeply feel your concern for the patient. Visualize your love being sent to the patient from your heart as a white laser beam of light. This is God's healing energy in prayer. As you do so, pray aloud:

God, let your healing power fill and heal _____. Let this healing begin now and continue until _____is well. Thank you for the healing that is now taking place. Amen.

Other Healing Resources

Traveling to these resources will supplement the daily healing efforts taking place in your home.

7) A Prayer Group

Groups can be found in churches, hospitals, and other places offering meeting space. The energy for healing in prayer groups derives from both the caring and the prayers. This is a process, not a one-step cure, so plan to attend regularly.

8) A Healing Service

You will find spiritual healing services in some churches of all faith traditions. All Church of the Brethren congregations offer healing services, as do all Pentecostal churches including the Church of God, Four Square Gospel, and Assemblies of God. Spiritualist churches always offer healing services. Feel free to phone a number of churches, and then find the one that feels right for you.

Science Fiction Time Travel Heals

You or a loved one might be able to travel into the past before your medical condition developed. Imagine yourself being in a certain previous year. When you are there, strengthen your energy fields so they are not susceptible to your upcoming medical condition. Do this in the same way you try to heal the physical body.

I observed a French Canadian do this successfully. When someone can do this, why can't you be another one to do it? If successful, your medical condition will disappear when you return to the present.

Practice this in this step or in chapters 21 or 22.

---

9) A Religious Service

When you walk in and feel surrounded by love, you have found the right church for healing. Sacred love produces healing.

10) A Time-Release Energy Capsule

I have created a time-release energy capsule dozens of times. Anytime you are finishing a healing session and you feel an especially strong flow of healing energy beneath your hand, bring your other hand close and cup your two hands together. Role your hands a circle in opposite directions to further increase the healing energy.

You may feel foolish as you create a
Time Release Energy Capsule but as you place it
in yourself, you can often feel its intense energy.

Then move your cupped hands to a place needing healing. Plant the energy there, while praying,

> *God, let this energy capsule release energy strongly over the next ___ hours. Thank you. Amen.*

The Ongoing Adventure

Please explore all the steps that follow this step. Each offers self-healing exercises that combine touch and prayer.

19

Physical Healing Session Models

These physical healing session models take you step-by-step through many conditions you may face. They are intended to guide you in healing yourself.

ALLERGIES & ASTHMA

Allergies and asthma respond well to healing efforts. Both have emotional roots. Following Emotional Release Therapy, most of my clients with allergies or asthma are cured. Therefore, self-healing is possible.

Whenever you are suffering from allergies or an asthma attack, practice Emotional Release Therapy. Release current anxieties. Release current emotional hurts. Go to your childhood and release emotionally painful memories associated with your parents. Also, release childhood fears of abandonment and being independent. In the midst of healing exercises one or two, intuitively ask yourself for the emotional source of your medical condition, then release it during Emotional Release Therapy.

Try an exorcism. Just after practicing Emotional Release Therapy, let your eyes remain closed. Then, command the spirit of allergies or asthma to depart. The words are not important, but here is a model to guide you:

In God's name, I command the spirit of allergies (or asthma) to depart from me. I no longer need you. I choose to be free. Leave me that I might be healthy and at peace. Let this begin now. Thank you, God. Amen.

Be patient. Repeatedly practice these two approaches.

ARTHRITIS

Arthritis is one of easiest conditions to heal. Following healing treatment, all symptoms of the arthritis will disappear within forty-eight hours. There will be no swelling, no pain, and full joint movement.

Arthritis does have an emotional component. So begin the healing session with Emotional Release Therapy. Release the emotional states of boredom, meaninglessness, and depression

Then remove the trauma memories of each arthritic joint. Pray: *God, remove the trauma memories from this joint. Thank you. Amen.* Afterwards, hold your healing hand about a quarter inch above the joint for about one minute each.

Then, spend about six minutes healing each joint. Pray: *God, heal this joint. Remove the pain and restore all tissue to normal. Thank you. Amen.* Use both hands, placing your hands on either side of the joint for about three minutes. Then reverse the hand positions for another three minutes. Repeat this procedure twice a day for three days.

For ten minutes each, charge several cotton dish towels with healing energy, using both hands. Place these towels on the worst arthritic joints twenty-four hours a day. Rubber bands work, but don't use tight ones that hamper circulation.

BURNS

For a superficial, first-degree burn, such as one from a baking pan, begin the healing treatment immediately:

Remove the emotional trauma from your heart (1 minute).
Remove the cellular trauma (half a minute).
Place your healing hand close to the burn. Pray for God to heal it (2 minutes). Healing charge any ointment before applying.

For severe third-degree burns caused by such things as a motorcycle exhaust pipe, a house fire, or ignited fuel:

Remove the emotional trauma from your heart (3 minutes).
Remove the cellular trauma from the burned flesh. From about half an inch away from the skin, move your healing hand above all burned areas to remove body trauma. Imagine your hand is a magnet removing the pain. Pray:

God, let my hand remove the pain and chaos from my body. Let the cells be at peace and reflect God's healing and ordered purpose to bring health to every cell. Begin regenerating healthy flesh. Let this happen quickly. This is an emergency. Thank you. Amen.

Whatever medium is used to soothe the burned areas, charge it with healing energy. For example, if you are soaked in an oil bath, take a quart of that oil and charge it with healing energy. Do so by holding the container between your hands and praying, *God fill this fluid with your healing power. Thank you. Amen.* Hold the container of fluid in your hands for ten minutes. Then pour that fluid into your larger bath. It will charge the whole bath with healing energy. Any soothing medium can be made healing charged in this way. If you are in shock, it still works.

Find an area of the skin that is unburned and use this area for the conducting of healing energy throughout your body. Do so by touching the skin and offering healing prayer, such as:

God, heal me. Speed up the normal healing process. Stop the pain. Restore my vital signs. Grant me your peace, presence and love. Thank you. Amen.

CANCER

Cancer responds well to Emotional Release Therapy, followed by healing touch and prayer.

Practice Emotional Release Therapy. Release all painful memories for the three years prior to the onset of your cancer. Focus upon painful losses: deaths, divorce, betrayals, separations, job losses, and physical, emotional, and sexual abuses. Focus on unhappy family and job relationships. Release anxiety, fear, anger, and depression. Practice Emotional Release Therapy daily.

If you live with a spouse or family, practice steps in Chapters 14 or 15.

Use healing charged materials. Charge a gallon of water with healing energy and drink two ounces four times a day. Charge cotton dish towels with healing energy. Place them on major cancer areas twenty-four hours a day.

Daily practice Healing Exercise #1 or #2.

Practice each of these for at least three months. By then, you should be able to accurately assess your results.

CHRONIC FATIGUE

Chronic fatigue responds well to Emotional Release Therapy.

Practice Emotional Release Therapy daily for a week. You are a very competent person who does everything well. But you are not getting the emotional support you need. Release your relational frustration. You also have painful memories associated with loved ones. Release them.

Use healing charged water. Charge a gallon of water with healing energy and drink two ounces four times a day.

Within a week, your fatigue and any other accompanying medical conditions will be gone. You will be your own energetic self again.

CROHN'S DISEASE

Practice Emotional Release Therapy daily for a month.

Use healing charged water. Charge a gallon of water with healing energy and drink two ounces four times a day. Do this for a month.

You should be symptom-free within a week but you are not cured. At the end of a month, try skipping treatment. If your Crohn's symptoms return, continue the above regimen.

We may not be able to cure Crohn's Disease, but we can eliminate the symptoms. You may have to continue the above process for the rest of your life. But you will live a normal, healthy life.

DENTAL PROCEDURE

Spiritual healing alleviates the after symptoms of dental care.

Before going to the dentist, place your hands on your jaws and practice healing prayer and touch. Pray:

> God, while at the dentist, protect me from pain and discomfort. Keep my gums and nerves healthy and nurture them during the dental procedure. Afterwards, restore my mouth and make it immediately healthy. Thank you. Amen.

Afterwards, again practice healing prayer and touch on your jaws.

If you are having a tooth removed, give the tooth permission to leave your jaw.

GENITAL HERPES

Practice Emotional Release Therapy daily for a week.

Use healing charged water. Charge a gallon of water with healing energy and drink two ounces four times a day for a week.

By the end of the week, your genital herpes should be gone. If not, repeat the above process for two more weeks.

HEART ATTACK

Remove the trauma in your heart muscle. Place your healing hand over your heart. Tell your heart to release the shock of the heart attack into your hand. Let this shock enter your hand. Then place your hand on your heart and pray, *God, let my heart be at peace. Thank you. Amen.* Let your hand remain there for a minute.

Practice touch-healing prayer on your heart. Touch your heart with your healing hand. Pray, *God restore life to my heart muscles. Regenerate and make them whole. Thank you. Amen.* Let your hand remain there for ten minutes. Do this three times a day.

Go through steps in chapter 9, Coping with a Scary Diagnosis.

Practice Emotional Release Therapy daily for a week and then weekly for six months.

Use healing charged water. Charge a gallon of water with healing energy and drink two ounces four times a day.

Use a healing charged cotton dishtowel. Charge it and place it on your heart twenty-four hours a day.

INFECTIONS

Bacterial and viral infections respond well to healing. Massive infections usually respond better than small ones. Remember two things: bacteria and viruses are living organisms with a consciousness; and the infected tissue is being traumatized by the infectious agents.

Whether the infection is small or massive, proceed this way:

Exorcism. Talk to the infectious agent. Say, *I neither need nor want this infection. Go away. In God's name, depart from me. Enter the light and be gone. Thank you, God. Amen*

Remove the trauma from your body tissue. Wherever you are feeling the most symptoms of distress, place your hand. Talk to your body. Tell it to release its discomfort into your hand. Tell it to be at peace.

Practice Emotional Release Therapy daily. Emotional pain or destructive emotional states have weakened your immune system and let the infection take over.

Charge bottle water. Charge a container of water with healing energy and drink two ounces every hour.

MULTIPLE SCLEROSIS

Multiple Sclerosis took a long time to develop and it takes a long healing process.

Practice Emotional Release Therapy daily.

Charge bottled water. Charge a container of water with healing energy and drink two ounces four times a day.

You should start feeling stronger within a week. Maintain this daily regimen for eighteen months.

MUSCLE INJURY

A sprained ankle, swollen knee, and torn tendons all respond well to touch-healing prayer.

Remove the emotional trauma from your heart (1 minute).

Remove the cellular trauma from the injured area (1 minute).

Place one or both hands around the injured area. Pray:

God, remove the pain and heal this injury with your healing power. Thank you. Amen.

For ten minutes, charge a cotton dishtowel with healing energy. Place that towel on the injured area. Use your own ingenuity to fasten it there. Leave the towel there twenty four hours a day until the injury is healed. The healing charged towel will constantly trickle healing energy into the wounded area.

The same healing procedure can be used for all other trauma injuries.

SHINGLES

Practice Emotional Release Therapy daily. Ask yourself why you need to have shingles. Release the emotions behind that need.

Remove the pain trauma from the most painful tissue.

Place your healing hand on the worst area of pain and pray for healing. Afterwards, leave your hand there for fifteen minutes.

Charge a bottle of water with healing energy. Drink two ounces four times a day.

All symptoms will be gone within a week.

SUNBURN

Before going out into the sun, apply sunshade. Begin by holding the sunshade container in your hand and charging it with healing energy before you apply it.

Treat sunburn as soon as you come in from the sun. If you begin hurting several hours later, healing touch still works.

First, go over the sunburned area with your healing hand about a quarter inch above the skin. Intend to remove the trauma from your skin cells. Pray:

God, remove the trauma from my skin. Let my hands act as a magnet in drawing it out.

Second, place your healing hand on red skin areas, about one minute per area. Pray:

God, heal this skin. Remove the damage and restore this skin to normal. Thank you. Amen.

Hold the salve container in your hand and charge it with healing energy for one minute. Then place the salve on your sunburn. This should work wonders.

20

Healing in a Medical Center

Can prayer help your diagnostic test results improve?

Why does prayer produce miracles during surgical procedures?

Would you like to be bathed in prayer while in a critical care unit?

Hospital stays are not like they used to be. Most diagnostic tests and surgical procedures are now done on an outpatient basis, during a few hours in a medical center. If you are admitted to the hospital, you are likely very sick. Your medical situation may be so acute that you are admitted to a critical care unit. Most of your Emotional Release Therapy and spiritual healing efforts, therefore, will take place in your home.

This chapter focuses on your preparations for a hospital visit and your needs as an outpatient or a patient.

Prayers During Diagnostic Tests

More families have told me of prayer healing miracles during diagnostic testing than in any other hospital setting. Usually it is the prayers of anxious parents that produce the prayer miracles.

My sister, Gayle, can attest to her experience. Her fourteen-year-old son, Chuck, for several months had had the symptoms of and had been diagnosed as having a devastating nerve disease that was inevitably fatal.

While Chuck was undergoing further diagnostic testing, Gayle and her husband, Charles, prayed. During their prayers, Chuck's obvious symptoms disappeared before the startled doctor's eyes and the subsequent diagnostic tests found Chuck to be in perfect health.

I know this is only an undocumented story, but I have heard dozens of similar stories and have taken part in dozens of others. When a loved one is being tested, the prayers of waiting family members produce amazing results.

1) A Prayer Before Diagnostic Testing

Ask loved ones to take your hands and pray with you the day *before* your diagnostic test. Provide this prayer model:

> *God, we are very worried about _____. He (or she) is having a diagnostic test that could discover a serious medical condition. In our loving concern, we ask you to heal _____ now. Remove the symptoms and the causes for them. Heal _____ and make him/her whole in body, mind, and spirit. Thank you for this healing. Amen.*

2) A Prayer During Diagnostic Testing

Since you are practicing self-healing, ask loved ones to soak you in prayer during your diagnostic test. Provide them with this prayer model and ask them to utilize the techniques which follow:

> *God, we are very worried about _____. In our loving concern, we ask you to heal _____ now. Remove the symptoms and the causes for them. Heal _____ and make him/her whole in body, mind, and spirit. Thank you for this healing. Amen.*

Continue bathing your loved one in prayer while using the following techniques.

Seek to form a spiritual oneness with the healee. Silently pray:

> *God, make me one with _____ in body, mind, and spirit. Bless this unity that it might produce wholeness.*

Mentally visualize the intended results while silently praying:

> *God, enable _____ to be restored into your perfect genetic image.*

Visualize twin objects and merge them into one, with one object representing you and the other the healee.

Another healing prayer:

> *God, fill _____ with your presence. Let this healing begin now and continue until complete health is attained. Thank you for the healing that is now taking place. Amen.*

3) Your Own Prayer Before Surgery

Begin offering this prayer about twenty-four hours before surgery. It will bring you inner calm, increase the oxygen in your blood by about ten percent, and cause all your tissue and organs to respond well to surgery.

Before praying, place your hands close to the surgical area. If this is not possible, place your dominant hand on your heart and the other on your diaphragm. Now pray:

God, I thank you for the upcoming surgery that will permit my body to heal itself. I thank you for the skills of each member of the surgical team. Guide them as they begin the healing of my body. Thank you.

God, I want to be well again. I pray that you will use me as a channel for my own healing. Let your healing energy flow into the surgical area and into my lungs and heart. Fill these areas with your life energy and increase the oxygen levels in my tissues.

Enable all the cells of my body to fight for health. Protect me from pain and bleeding during surgery and afterwards. Enable the surgical wound to heal quickly. Fill me with the calm and power of your presence. I open myself to a oneness with you. I rest in your care and wisdom. Thank you. Amen.

4) A Prayer with Loved Ones Before Surgery

Ask one or more loved ones to pray with you before surgery. Ask that this be done twenty-four hours before and then just before surgery. If one person participates, the two of you hold hands. If more, have everyone touch your body some place during prayers. Here is a pre-surgical prayer model for your loved ones to use:

God, we thank you for _____ and what he or she means to us. In our love, we are concerned.

Let our hands flow with your healing power, that _____ might be filled with your life-giving energy so that he glows with your sacredness. Fill _____ with your love and peace.

Begin healing his/her medical condition right now. Heal _____ in body, mind, and spirit.

During surgery, may every tissue in his/her body cooperate for _____'s health. Maintain his/her vital signs, let his/her heart and lungs be strong, and protect _____ from pain and bleeding. Let his/her surgical wound heal quickly.

Inspire and guide the medical team, that they may do their best professional work.

Be with each of us as we stand vigil for _____ while he or she is in surgery. Thank you. Amen.

Ask your loved ones to all pray together for you in these ways while you are in surgery:

Seek to form a spiritual oneness with the healee. Silently pray:

God, make me one with _____ in body, mind, and spirit. Bless this unity that it might produce wholeness.

Mentally visualize the intended results, silently praying:

God, let _____ be healed even as the surgery progresses.

Visualize twin objects and merge them into one, with one object representing you and the other the healee.

A surgery prayer:

God, fill _____ with your love and light. Provide for his/her needs and protect him/her from all harm. Thank you for the healing and wholeness that you are creating in _____ right now. Amen.

5) Loved Ones' Prayer - Critical Care Unit

If you should enter a critical care unit, ask loved ones to touch and pray for you personally within the unit.

Outside the unit, they can find a quiet place to gather for prayer. This setting is one in which many instant healings take place. Their anxiety is a powerful expression of love. Alter the previous prayer model to fit this situation.

6) Your Prayer During a Hospital Stay

Before beginning, place your hands on the affected area. If you do not know what needs to be healed, place your dominant hand on your heart and the other on your diaphragm.

God, I am thankful to be in this hospital where I am receiving the special care I need. I am thankful for the doctors, nurses, and others who are here to help me. Guide and sustain them as they care for me.

Grant me the wisdom to make the right decisions about my care. Keep me safe and enable me to return home soon in the process of becoming whole.

God, be with me as I now practice Emotional Release Therapy on myself by choosing a color to symbolize my emotional pain and stress. I now release that color, a symbol of all my emotional pain, into my dominant hand on my heart.

Take all the time you need to do this, for your hurts may be contributing to your medical condition. Then, leave your dominant hand on your heart and continue praying.

God, let your love and peace flow from my hand and into my heart, filling me with your presence. Thank you.

God, heal me in body, mind, and spirit. Begin the healing that I need and let it continue until I am well. Thank you for the healing that is taking place through-

*out my whole being. I accept it with deep apprecia-
tion. Amen.*

7) Your Own Ongoing Touch-Healing Prayer

Place one or both hands on either side of the area
needing to be healed. Or place your dominant hand on
your heart and the other on your diaphragm. Do this for
ten minutes at a time, morning, afternoon and evening
as you pray:

*God, use my hands as channels for your healing
love, so that wherever I place my hands, your healing
flow enters and heals me. May this healing begin now
and continue until I am well. Thank you. Amen.*

21

Meditative Prayer
Healing Exercise #1

If you master these procedures and stay with them for several weeks, meditative prayer will become a joy for you. You are motivated by your focus on becoming well. You will also become the beneficiary of a number of pleasing side effects. Meditative prayer slowly produces changes in you.

Meditation is a secular mental exercise that sharpens your brain functioning and guides you toward emotional wholeness. When a religious context is added to meditation, it deepens your contact with God. Meditative prayer produces optimal functioning of the mental, emotional, and spiritual energy fields, which then affect the physical energy field, producing physical healing.

Daily meditation quiets random thoughts and emotions. The chatter in your brain grows silent. If you choose to think nothing, there is silence. You mentally gain control of your thinking and emotions. Your ability to concentrate, remember, and create increases dramatically. Barriers to action are removed. Procrastination ends. You set a goal and find yourself easily acting to accomplish it. You sleep more soundly, feeling refreshed in the morning.

Meditative prayer provides more energy. An inner sense of calm begins to pervade you. You become more able to choose how you would like to feel. Your emotional responses become more spontaneous and vital. Painful buried memories and emotions surface, not to hurt, but to be healed.

You develop the ability to study a situation or problem from an emotional distance. You lower stress levels. In doing so, you may lower your pulse and blood pressure, as well.

Prayerful meditation can strengthen the reality of your religious beliefs. It can transform you into your image of God and empower this divine image within you. It can heal both life's hurts and those of the physical body.

You will find some exercises easier for you than others. Just because an exercise is difficult does not mean you cannot and should not master it. Mastering the difficult exercise may fulfill your greatest need. Try every exercise at least twice before choosing those parts that are most helpful for you. Before beginning, warm up with this imaging skill exercise.

Visualizing. Forming a picture in the mind and holding it is hindered by strong effort. It happens best through passive action. To practice mental imaging, place a simple object before you. Look at it. Close your eyes and form a mental picture. Hold that image as long as possible; only a few seconds may be likely at the beginning. Then repeat this process again and again.

Suggested images: *Simple:* An orange, an apple, a ball, a color (such as green, red, blue, yellow.) *More complex:* a chair, a table, a kitchen appliance, a tree, a flower, an animal. *Advanced:* an entire room, a familiar human face.

Meditative Prayer Healing Exercise #1
Being Healed by God

Find a quiet place in a calming light. You may need to maintain one position for up to an hour, so find a comfortable place to sit or to lie down with your back straight. This should be a place set apart from the responsibilities and business of the world. Arrange not to be disturbed. Quiet the phone.

Focus solely upon what you are about to do. Have a timer present so you will not have to keep track of time yourself. Hold these instructions on your lap or in a hand so you can follow them conveniently. You might want to ask someone to lead you through the instructions the first time.

Are you comfortable? Move around until you are confident of your comfort. Breathe deeply and relax. With repetition, this process will move smoothly.

---

1) A *Self-Relaxing Exercise (Autogenic Training)*

The purpose of this exercise is to place you in a relaxed state similar to hypnosis. To accomplish this, you will be moving and flexing various muscle groups. These actions make you aware of each area. Then you will be telling each body part that it will relax as you count from ten down to one. This procedure worked for me the first time I attempted it, but it can take a dozen trials before it works.

Right Leg: Flex once the muscle groups of your right leg—your toes, foot, ankle, calf, thigh, and buttocks. Then silently speak to your right leg:

> *As I count from ten down to one, my right leg is going to relax, beginning with the tip of the toes and flowing right up through the foot, the ankle, the calf, the knee, the thigh, the buttocks. This relaxation will feel like a heaviness or tingling.*

Then, while breathing slowly and deeply on each inhalation and exhalation, count silently:

> *Ten, nine, eight, seven, six, five, four, three, two, one.*

Then silently say,

> *My right leg is now relaxing and will continue to relax as I proceed. Then proceed to the left leg.*

Left Leg: Repeat the instructions given for the right leg.

Torso: Flex the muscles of the lower back, middle back, upper back, shoulders, rib cage, diaphragm and belly. Then silently speak to your torso:

> *As I count from ten to one, my torso is going to relax, beginning with my lower back, up my back to my shoulders and then down the front through my rib cage, diaphragm and tummy. All my internal organs are being relaxed—my heart, lungs, liver, stomach, intestines, bladder, and kidneys.*

Then, while breathing slowly and deeply on each inhalation and exhalation, count silently:

Ten, nine, eight, seven, six, five, four, three, two, one.

Then say,

My torso is now relaxing and will continue to relax as I proceed.

Right Arm: Flex once the muscle groups of your right arm—your fingers, hand, wrist, forearm, elbow, and biceps. Then silently speak to your right arm:

As I count from ten to one, my right arm is going to relax, beginning with the tips of my fingers and flowing up my arm to my shoulder. This relaxation will feel like a heaviness or a tingling.

Then, while breathing slowly and deeply on each inhalation and exhalation, count silently:

Ten, nine, eight, seven, six, five, four, three, two, one. Then silently say, My right arm is now relaxing and will continue to relax as I proceed.

Left Arm: Repeat the same procedure as on the right arm.

Neck and Head: Flex the muscles in your neck, throat, jaw, cheeks, forehead, temples, scalp. Then say,

As I count from ten to one, my neck and throat, jaws and cheeks, forehead, temples and scalp are going to relax.

Then, while breathing slowly and deeply on each inhalation and exhalation, count silently:

Ten, nine, eight, seven, six, five, four, three, two, one.

Final Countdown: This time do not flex any muscles. As you count from ten to one, sense all the muscle groups, beginning with the right leg. Sense, and then quietly tell each muscle group to relax. Say:

*As I count from ten to one, each muscle group I
tell to relax will relax even further, doubling my state
of relaxation. Then count silently: ten, nine, eight,
seven, six, five, four, three, two, one.*

2) Entering the Mystical Room

You are now unclothed and have an imaginary body.
Let your imaginary body stand up. Before you is a
doorway. As you look through the doorway, you see
steps leading downward.

The steps are well lit and covered with purple carpet.
You are going to walk down these steps and, as you do
so, you will find yourself going deeper into your mind.

There are twenty steps. As you walk down the steps,
you will count each of the twenty steps. One, two, three...

You are now at the bottom of the steps. Before you is
a room, a mystical room. It has white walls, white ceiling,
and white carpet. In the center of the room is a white
chair. Walk to the chair and be seated. In this chair, you
have complete access to God.

3) Being with God

Seek out God. Sense his immensity. Be filled with the
sweetest, purest love you have ever known— God. Sit
quietly and enjoy God's presence. Then wait silently,
listening for God's voice to speak to you.

4) God's Cleansing

When you are ready, you feel a mist of warm rain
falling upon you. The rain is God cleansing you. The rain

enters the top of your head and flows through all parts of your body. Every organ and cell the rain touches represents God cleansing and purifying you.

Let the rain cleanse your mind and all your thoughts and feelings. Let it flow into the chest cavity and cleanse your heart and lungs, your liver and stomach, and each organ of your body.

Let it flow through your arms and out your fingers, through your legs and out through your toes. You are being cleansed and made pure as God touches every part of you.

5) God's Healing Light

The rain has stopped. You have been purified. You are now ready to be healed by God's healing white light.

As you sit in your white chair, you sense a warmth like that of the sun bathing you. It is not the sun, but rather a shaft of God's healing light. The white healing light enters your body through the top of your head. You welcome the warmth and love as God's healing light slowly begins flowing throughout your mind, healing it.

God is recreating you and making every part of you new and healthy. You let the healing light slowly flow throughout your body, healing every organ and cell.

Eventually, the healing light flows down your arms and out through your fingers, then down through your torso, down your legs, and out through your toes. Every cell in your body has been renewed. You sense your energy fields, filled with healing energy, radiating in a strong and balanced fashion.

6) God Empowers Your Hands

God calls your name:

_____, your hands are now filled with the power of my healing flow. Your hands now radiate the power of my love. Lift your hands and move them over your body, pausing at places that need special healing.

This is a double blessing of healing. You feel the healing flow radiating from your hands and entering every cell, regenerating and making all things new. You sense the healing taking place.

You rejoice in the healing. You now feel so light, you feel that you could float. You are being restored . . . .

Then pray:

7) A Prayer for Healing

God, out of love you created the universe and made it good. You created human beings in your own image, meaning that we are spiritual beings like yourself. You granted me the gift of life. You have traveled with me throughout my life's journey. Thank you.

Now place your dominant hand on your heart and practice Radiant Heart Therapy. Choose a color symbol and on the cue begin.

God, I wish to reclaim your perfect image. Help me to touch your presence within me. I release into my hand my pains and my hurts, my worries and my fears to your care. I release to you all my negative thoughts, attitudes, feelings. I relax and place myself in your hands. You are the potter and I am the clay. God, cleanse my inner being and mold me into your love.

When you have finished Emotional Release Therapy, with your dominant hand still on your heart, fill yourself with God, according to the following words of prayer:

God, let your love flow into my heart through my hand. Now let your Spirit, your power, your presence flow into my heart through my hand. Fill me with spiritual bliss.

Let my whole being be filled with and glow with your light. Let my energy fields reflect your perfect power and form. Let every cell of my body be renewed by your beauty and magnificence.

Let me know perfect health. I accept the healing that is coursing through me. I accept your healing in body, mind, and spirit. I choose to be well, vibrant and fully alive. I sense your wholeness filling me. Thank you.

God, bless me that I might become a blessing to you. Show me a vision of what you see me becoming. Fill me with a heart of wisdom. Thank you for the joy that has filled me. I rest in your love. Amen.

8) Closing

Take your time. When you are ready, leave the mystical room. Arise and walk to the stairway. Climb the steps, counting each of twenty steps as you do so. Return to your body.

Tell yourself, *When I count from one to three, I will be back in my normal state. One, two three.*

You now feel refreshed and renewed. You now feel whole. This may or may not be reflected in a complete physical healing.

If you found this meditative prayer process helpful, then practice it every day.

A similar meditative prayer process is offered in the next chapter.

Following six weeks of this type of meditative prayer, I had a peak experience of God that completely restored my damaged heart muscle.

May you soon be surprised with your own healing.

22

Meditative Prayer
Healing Exercise #2

To understand the benefits of meditative prayer, return to Chapter 21.

Find a quiet place with a calming light. You may need to maintain one position for up to an hour, so find a comfortable place to sit or to lie down with your back straight. This is a place set apart from the responsibilities and business of the world. Arrange not to be disturbed. Quiet the phone.

Focus solely upon what you are about to do. Have a timer present so you will not have to keep track of time yourself. Hold these instructions on your lap or in a hand so you can conveniently follow them. You might ask someone to lead you through the instructions the first time.

Breathe deeply through your nostrils and relax. With repetition, this whole process will move smoothly.

1) Centering

If possible, begin by standing and gently stretching and flexing every muscle in your body while inhaling and exhaling deeply through the nostrils down into your diaphragm. Do so three times.

Let's begin. Inhale-stretch and flex-exhale. Inhale-stretch and flex-exhale. Inhale-stretch and flex-exhale. Now sit straight or lie down on your back.

2) A Focusing or Mantra Meditation

In this focusing, sit or lie with your eyes closed and repeat a word or phrase aloud for ten minutes. Let the pauses between speaking take about the same time as the speaking. Make no attempt to think about the meaning of what you are saying; just say it.

You will have distractions. These commonly include an itching nose or cheek, the hardness of the seat pressing into your buttocks or back, your mind wandering to something you have to do, or thinking through something.

These are your mind's attempts to interrupt your focus. Ignore them and gently bring your focus back to speaking your word or phrase over and over. It is the attempt which counts, not your perfection in doing it. **Your instructions are these:**

Choose a word or short phrase to say. Suggestions:

Love, Peace, God, One, All is One, God is Love, Grant me your peace, Be still and know that I am God.

Set your timer for ten minutes.

Begin.

Then, move on to the next exercise.

3) Imaging Relaxation

When the mind relaxes, the body also relaxes. Here you will imagine that you are relaxing alone in a secluded outdoor place such as a warm sunny beach. Set your timer for at least four minutes.

You are alone in your bathing suit on a secluded, warm, sunny beach. You lie down and feel the sun gently warming your skin.

Close your eyes. You have taken a vacation from worries and responsibilities. You are at peace with yourself and the world. You can hear birds singing and the water is lapping at the shore. Just relax and be. The present moment is filled with love and peace.

Stay as long as you want. Then, proceed.

4) The Meditation of Breath Counting

Close your eyes and, while breathing normally, count your exhalations in your mind in groups of four.

Inhale-exhale-one, inhale-exhale-two, inhale-exhale-three, inhale-exhale-four, then repeat inhale-exhale-one, etc.

Begin with five minutes and work up to fifteen minutes. Use a timer. While doing this meditation, seek to keep your mind free of all physical awareness, thoughts, and feelings.

5) Waterfall Cleansing

Imagine a waterfall of sparkling water at a comfortable temperature. Enter the waterfall unclothed or in a bathing suit.

Imagine the water entering your body through the top of your head. Let it flow throughout your body, beginning with your head, down your arms and out your fingers, through your torso, down your legs and out your toes. Imagine the water cleansing every organ it touches. Take your time.

6) *God's Healing Light*

Think of the most loving person you know. Imagine this person placing his or her hand on the top of your head. He or she says: "In the name of God, be healed!"

You sense the love of God surrounding and entering you. You feel the healing white light of God pervading your body from his or her hand.

Let it bathe your whole being. Sense it surrounding and entering every organ of your body. Let it surround every area where there is illness.

Wherever God's healing light touches, say: I *am being healed.*

God's healing white light is now regenerating your body, mind, and spirit.

7) *Your Own Healing Hands*

Place your hands on areas needing to be healed. Pray:

God, use my hands as channels for your healing power. Wherever I touch, the healing energy is regenerating and renewing me. I am being healed. Thank you. Amen.

8) *Imaging Wholeness*

You are as you believe. Imagine you have been healed and you are now taking part in joyous physical situations. See yourself dancing, biking, running, playing, creating, being vigorously alive, healthy and happy.

9) Centering On God

Now quiet your mind. Sense your inner calm. Be open to any message which may come to you. This is contemplation.

10) Closing Prayer

God, Creator, Sustainer, Healer, thank you for the hope that wells up within me. Thank you for the healing that has begun and continues to restore my body, mind and soul.

I accept this healing because I want to be well. Continue to fill me with your presence, with your love, joy and peace, that I might continue to have faith and trust in your care. Amen.

Conclusion

The differences between Meditative Prayer Healing Exercises #1 and #2 are immense. The two approaches serve different needs.

Exercise #1 uses Autogenic Training to place you in a relaxed state and then takes you on a spiritual journey that appeals to the emotions.

In contrast, Exercise #2 uses meditative exercises to relax you, then takes you on a mental journey that ends with spiritual imaging.

Using both balances your needs.

Background music. I have created cassettes that use appropriate background music for each exercise, including ocean surf for the beach meditation. Your experience may be enhanced adding your own subdued background music.

The Next Step

Aside from meditative prayer, there are many other ways to alter your consciousness. Any time that you shift your state of consciousness holds the possibility of producing a cure for your disease.

In Chapter 23, you are offered some of these possibilities.

I have personally tried most of the cited shifts in consciousness. I have had several motivations for doing so. First, I have felt led to research for any means for bringing healing to sick people. Second, I have wondered if any of these might be a key for a deeper experience of God. Finally, I have been curious.

Using any of them is your choice.

23

A Shift in Consciousness

Accumulated scientific evidence indicates that any time a person is able to achieve a peak state of consciousness, personal transformation and empowerment can occur. This outcome includes emotional and physical healing.

Using biofeedback, you can learn to enter the low theta brain wave state of four to eight frequencies per second. At that point, you get into a state of consciousness where you can move up and go into a state of revelry. This state is called the autogenic shift. You are operating at the back of the head in the left cortex or the left occipital lobe of the brain.

Elmer Green, who set up the Psychophysiology Lab at the Menninger Clinic in Topeka, Kansas, reports that through biofeedback a Westerner can attain the mystic state of the Tibetan or Hindu yogi in two to three days. The body, emotions, and thoughts are quieted as you enter the unconscious upper four levels of consciousness. This is known as self-mastery.

At this consciousness level, you can focus your intentions downward for the transformation of the body, emotions, and thoughts. When alcoholics get into this theta state, they can turn their attention downwards to the hypothalamus area of the brain. They are able to rewire that gland so that they no longer want to drink. This has been successfully done with 6,000 alcoholic subjects to date.

The limbic area of the brain is the emotional brain. The limbic area of the brain must have activity in it for us to feel emotions in our physical bodies. The emotions are connected to our unconscious, so we enter the unconscious through the limbic area.

Dr. Green states, "Sensory information from the outer world enters through the limbic brain which is the master of the mechanical brain which is the master of the body. If you take the information from the body and put it back into the outside world—that is biofeedback—and you look at it and you imagine what you would like to happen—the limbic brain is not smart enough to know that what you are imagining is not the real thing. It responds to it as if it were information of your sensory perceptions of outside the skin events, acting as if it were the real thing.

"The body responds to our visualizations as if they were the real thing—the real world. That is the power of visualization. The reason visualization works is because the limbic system implements it—controlling the hypothalamus, the pituitary and the physiological responses. All you have to do is get some feedback and you can learn to control it.

"There is a spectrum of consciousness from sleep, delta (1-4 bps [brain-waves per second]), to theta (4-8 bps), to alpha (8-13 bps), to beta or wide awake (13-26 bps). If you get into a state of consciousness where you can move UP and go into revelry, you can go into this state called the autogenic shift. You are in theta (4-8 bps) and at the back of the head in the left cortex or the left occipital lobe—a visual lobe. It is also concerned with analysis or reasoning. You have to be awake, in beta, to analyze. You cannot analyze very well in alpha and not at all in theta. If you can get the left cortex, the visual part, to go into theta, then you free the rest of the brain to do some very interesting things.

"I am talking about yoga—deep Tibetan yoga, deep Hindu yoga—that is what it is all about. A yogi is sitting there getting his body quiet, getting his emotions quiet, getting his thoughts quiet. When that happens, people go into theta.

"In theta brain-wave training, people are able to develop this profound trance-like state in Westerners in two to three days. The reason it works so quickly is that, by meditation alone, you do not know exactly when you are in the theta state.

In biofeedback, when the tone beeps, you know you are in theta. If, when the tone beeps, you say, 'Oh, I am in theta,' then you are no longer in theta. You cannot have theta when you mentally know it is there. [When you use the mental rational state of consciousness, theta disappears and you return to beta.] In order to be at theta and notice it is there, you have to become a witness—a witness above yourself to transcend your normal self—above your body, emotions and thoughts."

When you get the body, emotions and thoughts quiet, you find that you are still here. You are at the entrance to the mystic state—the white light—and at that point, you can focus the intentions downward, and you can start to get the body, emotions, and thoughts under control.

Many of the biofeedback subjects, without knowing anything about it ahead of time, experience a tunnel. They can have OBEs (Out of Body Experiences.) One subject said, "I felt like I had electricity shooting out of the top of my head. I saw this bright light on the other side. I realized I had to go there. I started running down the tunnel and I saw the light coming from a figure of me. It was upside down and on top of another figure of me. [That is the temple with the angels and the demons.] The light was so intense it was too painful to continue." Those who have this experience have difficulty putting it into words. This is the ineffable zone. But you know it without words.

Those who work with LSD have been able to get up there and go through, but they could not stay up there because it was a chemically-induced shot, and inevitably they came back to earth, with no helpful outcome.

Biofeedback research provides the scientific data and rationale needed for us to trust altered states of consciousness as a reliable means for achieving health and wholeness. Similar claims for hypnosis, autogenic training, visualization, and meditation are also validated by biofeedback research.

1) Biofeedback Theta Training

You may want to use biofeedback on your own path back to health. The first step is finding someone certified in biofeedback theta training. Many college psychology departments have a certified theta biofeedback professor. Some hospitals use theta biofeedback. You might find biofeedback theta training among psychologists, psychiatrists, or physicians. If not, these sources may refer you to someone. Try the Yellow Pages of your phone book.

2) Hypnosis

Hypnosis was the first technique used to reprogram the brain. During the 1950s, German psychiatrist Johannes Schultz became convinced that hypnosis could be used to control the cortical and subcortical brain processes. He helped patients visualize their way back to health. With hypnosis, Schultz produced many of the results that have since been clinically verified in biofeedback training.

This approach was hampered by the human problem. People did not want to be hypnotized. So Schultz developed a self-help technique, Autogenic Training, that people could induce for themselves. This produced results similar to those of hypnosis. You used Autogenic Training in Chapter 21.

While one is in a hypnotic state, suggestion can program the brain. A professional hypnotist can program you to regularly enter a hypnotic state through post-hypnotic suggestion involving a triggering word, enabling you to do your own suggesting and visualization.

Elmer Green suggests that you can make all kinds of things happen in the body through hypnosis. All you need is an "Organ Specific Formula"—directions fitting your specific condition.

3) Autogenic Training

In 1975, I used Autogenic Training as the basis for healing my damaged heart muscle. Once in this self-induced state, you must employ a conscious technique. I used meditation, visualization, and prayer for more than an hour daily for six weeks. Within two weeks, I was completely relaxed, with my stress and fear replaced by inner calmness. In the sixth week, I had a peak experience of God that included perceiving a brilliant white light in my mind, during which my heart muscle was healed. This experience also involved touch-healing, as my own hands on my chest produced an incredible amount of healing energy.

Through Autogenic Training, many people can produce within themselves the same phenomena found in subjects of hypnosis research. At the time of his research, Schultz's clinical findings were dismissed by most physicians and psychologists as placebo effects. Biofeedback researchers have now provided the physiological answers for why Autogenic Training works. Autogenic Training can be trusted to reprogram the brain and mind, just as do biofeedback and hypnosis.

When you see a bright white light in your brain, or a tunnel, you know you are in theta and can quickly reprogram the brain for health and wholeness. When you have a peak experience of God, the bright white light and the tunnel are usually missing, but you are still in the effective theta state of brain-wave activity needed for healing transformation and empowerment.

My experience confirms that during any noticeable religious experience, even if you are just short of theta, you are still quietly and slowly reprogramming the brain and mind over a period of time.

4) *Meditation*

To most people, meditation is a bore. But when combined with Autogenic Training, meditation flows far more easily. Daily meditation produces the theta state on its own.

Until recently, meditation, the traditional tool of Hindu yogis, Tibetan monks, and Christian mystics, has been thought of as only a religious endeavor. Using mental techniques, one concentrated upon the revealed image of God. The purpose was to draw closer to God and thus become more like the revealed image of God upon which one focused.

Now meditation is also seen as having the potential to bring about a shift of consciousness and lead one to wholeness and health. In this context, meditation involves focusing in such a way as to transform one's awareness or consciousness. It requires turning inward in concentration on those images and symbols that arise from our unconscious depths, as we pause for a time of silence or inner focus.

All meditation techniques produce the same results. Meditations as simple as breath-count-in, or repeating a word or phrase for twenty minutes, can produce all the results you are seeking.

5) *Visualizations and Affirmations*

Visualization and affirmations can also reprogram the brain and mind, but for that to occur, they must be done while in a spiritual state or in the alpha and theta states.

6) Brennan's Hara Dimension

In her book, *Light Emerging—the Journey of Personal Healing*, Barbara Ann Brennan breaks amazing new ground for our understanding of the healing and empowerment of the human energy fields.

The *hara* exists on a dimension deeper than the auric field. It is the source of your physical body's energy and of your manifestation as physical. The *tan tien* is the source of power in the martial arts, such as *tai chi*. It is also the source of power of all personal intention and life purpose. When the *tan tien* is healed, a person becomes energized and directed for creative, fulfilling living.

7) Near-Death Experience (NDE)

In a 1982 Gallup poll, about eight million Americans reported having had near-death experiences. The near-death experience is considered by researchers to be only a peak experience of God that proves the existence of an afterlife.

As a healing researcher, I have reached a different conclusion. A key element completely ignored by other researchers is that NDEs have resulted in the restoration of a clinically dead physical body. Thus, I am led to conclude that the real significance of an NDE is that it is a healing experience.

The perception of a white light or tunnel indicates that an NDE is a peak state of consciousness. Experiences are in the theta state, during which they can reprogram the brain/mind and be healed.

Elmer Green also identified the NDE as the theta state of peak consciousness. "People who have out-of-body experiences and near-death experiences—their brains are not working, but their minds and emotions are working."

8) Out-of-Body Experiences

One of my parishioners, Gib, struggled with multiple sclerosis for seven years. The disease had progressed to the point where he was bedridden, with his only loco- motion, as he said, "being to squirm across the floor like a snake."

One day, Gib experienced an instant miracle of heal- ing and was cured of his MS. Here is the story in Gib's own words:

"It was December. As Christmas music filled our home, my wife and her girlfriend were baking Christ- mas cookies. I was lying in bed as usual with my MS, savoring the smell of baking cookies as it wafted in from the kitchen. Suddenly, I found myself up at the ceiling looking down at my physical body on the bed. I was completely at peace. Then the strangeness of the situation sank in. I became fearful and found myself back in my body. I was so excited by what had happened that I wanted to tell my wife. Without thinking, I got out of bed and walked into the kitchen. Boy, was she shocked to see me! I hadn't walked in a year. Being curious, I had two different medical doctors examine me. Both could find no trace of the disease and called it a misdiagnosis."

Gib had had a spontaneous out-of-body experi- ence (OBE) in which one senses the mind or con- sciousness leaving one's physical body, often hovering at ceiling level, but capable of traveling quickly to almost any place.

History is replete with stories of spontaneous OBEs. Many report having OBEs, also known as astral travel or second-body travel, during sleep. Often, it is a once-in-a-lifetime experience arising from moments of great emotional stress or physical illness. Such an experience is definitely a peak state of consciousness that holds the potential for restoring the energy fields and the physical body through a shift in awareness. It is, therefore, another medium for healing miracles.

9) Laughter

One of the most celebrated cases of restored health produced by a shift in consciousness was reported by Norman Cousins. In his book, *Anatomy of an Illness*, Cousins describes how laughter, intention, and courage cured him of a serious collagen illness, a disease of the connective tissue.

10) Experiencing the Presence of God

Experiencing the sacred and the holy, and being touched by God, are transformative experiences. Any experience that produces an inner sense of awe, wonder, faith, hope, and love can produce inner wholeness. Make these available to yourself on a daily basis by drawing upon your own religious beliefs and practices.

11) Dreams and Visions

Throughout the centuries, literature has been filled with references to the dreams and visions of religious, political, military, scientific, artistic, and literary figures. With practice, one can learn to recall most dreams.

All dreams are meaningful and have purposes. Dreams are windows through which we can focus upon the subconscious mind and upon all the unresolved issues with which we have not consciously dealt. Dreams offer hope as they bid us to live life more fully than it is consciously lived in the daily awake state.

It is estimated that more than ninety percent of dream content is attempting to cope with unresolved personal issues. Thus, one path to wholeness lies in dream therapy or dream work. If one is struggling to survive, exploring one's dreams may lead one onto the path back to wholeness. This is especially helpful for persons seeking to recover from chemical addictions, neurotic behavior, depression, traumatic memories, and acute or chronic illnesses.

Procedure. Dream work is surprisingly simple, although it does require nightly preparations. If others sleep in your bedroom, plans must be made for not disturbing their sleep. Because dream content is quickly forgotten, it must be immediately recorded upon awakening. Keep a cassette recorder or paper and pen, plus a light, next to your bed. Before going to sleep, program yourself to remember dreams by saying something like: "I will begin remembering dreams tonight and will briefly awaken after each dream in order to record it. Then I will quickly fall back to sleep for further dreaming. I will awaken rested in the morning."

My personal experience is to awaken rested in the morning after having recorded four or five dreams. The first few nights you may recall few or no dreams. Be persistent. You will succeed. A fifteen-minute daily session of meditation facilitates dream recall.

Dreams come to us in symbolic pictures, sounds, and voices. Afterwards, one must interpret what these symbols mean. Trust your own personal understanding. Dreams may have a beginning, a middle conflict, and an end resolution. Many dreams are ordinary, dealing with daily inner and outer life issues. These dreams can provide helpful insight into the issues troubling us.

Anxiety dreams or nightmares cover areas of life in which we have not faced our fears.

Affirming dreams mirror new steps we are taking in our lives, or they support our present spiritual journey.

Intuitive-creative dreams can resolve real-life issues. Psychic dreams can forecast one's own or another's future—such as moving, getting a new job, becoming ill, becoming well. They may also become self-fulfilling prophecies when we choose to let them influence our future.

Another type of dream is a lucid dream. A lucid dream is so vividly real that we think it represents reality. Some persons have become capable of intervening in their own lucid dreams, controlling the ending, whether these endings involve anxiety, unresolved personal issues, or creativity.

Others report being able to program themselves on the content of their dreams. Before going to sleep, they say, "I need help with this issue in my life, so I ask that my dreams tonight deal with this issue. How can I get myself together?"

Persistent dream work over a six-week period of time can be a very rewarding path toward wholeness.

12) *Generous Love*

The receiving and the sharing of generous love leads to wholeness. In religion, this is known as divine love or *agape*. In secular terms, it is called *altruistic love*. Nothing leads to a change of consciousness and eventual wholeness more effectively than receiving and sharing a quality of love that liberates, empowers and restores.

Loving and serving others is great wellness therapy. The acts should be done with no expectation of wages or of being paid back. Acting as a volunteer caregiver serves this function.

13) *Falling in Love*

Romantically falling in love causes a shift in awareness. This experience is described as "being on cloud nine," or as "floating ten feet off the ground."

Falling in love is not reserved for singles. Marriages of all durations can experience this phenomenon. Genuine affection between persons releases an energy for healing. Expressions of sexual passion also energize and balance the human energy field while leading to a momentary shift in consciousness.

24

The Final Healing

Even with the best of understanding, intentions, and effort, your illness may result in death, the Final Healing. Our knowledge of healing prayer is still in its infancy. What we do know is that when we immerse ourselves in prayer, God enables us to face death with inner peace and serenity.

Skeptics of healing prayer ask the taunting question, "You do not expect to keep people alive forever with prayer, do you? We all die someday." My response is that no matter what the final outcome, the quality of life improves immensely through the use of healing prayer.

A Presbyterian minister told me how his wife faced spreading breast cancer. The medical prognosis was eighteen months. With healing prayer, a loving family, and the support of her religious community, she lived twelve years.

These were not closed-in years of waiting to die, filled with unhappiness, fear, and depression. They were joyous, satisfying years. She had worked through any feelings of fear, anger, and self-pity. She had faith and hope that God was with her in life, in death, and in life beyond death. She daily experienced God's presence, peace, and joy. She continued living a full life of caring love and warm, supportive relationships. Healing prayer prolonged her life and provided abundant living for both herself and her husband.

We are eternal and never die. Death is but a transition. In death, we sleep and awaken as though into the next morning. We find that the ravages of illness and aging have been erased. We are vital and whole once more, living in a spiritual body that is just as real as the physical body we left behind. There is joy and security in that knowledge.

Healing prayer produces a sense of God's power and presence within people. This is the most convincing personal evidence as the Unseen and the Eternal transform us into New Persons, able to live victoriously even to the moment of physical death.

Preparing for the Dying Process

Dying can become a lonely, isolated journey, or it can be a joyous and fulfilling journey shared with loved ones. Just as you have taken charge of your own emotional and physical healing, there is merit, should the need arise, in taking charge of your own dying process.

I observe that loved ones have a harder time facing death than does the dying person. Because people do not cope with dying often, they have little understanding of the process, and few coping skills.

Loved ones tend to avoid talking about death unless the dying person brings up the subject. There is often a conspiracy of silence about discussing the subject of death with the dying loved one.

Commonly there is complete avoidance, using the mechanism of false assurances, such as, "You are not dying. You are going to be all right. You will feel much better tomorrow. You are getting well." This can be maddening to the dying person who has sensed the truth.

During prolonged periods of dying, loved ones can work through their grief prematurely before the impending death occurs. In doing so, they emotionally separate themselves from the dying. To the dying, this comes through as, "My family no longer cares about me. They have already buried me and I no longer matter. I am all alone during the Final Healing."

Taking charge of your own dying process means that you do not play a passive role. You assert what you want from your loved ones. You bridge the gap of silence. You talk to loved ones about your own dying and death. You tend to their anguish and pain as well as your own. Talking to loved ones about your impending death provides courage, meaning and support for everyone. Here are some suggestions.

1) **Repeatedly state to loved ones:** "All the evidence points to the fact that I am closing in on death. It would be helpful to me if we talked about the issues involved. Are you willing to cooperate with me on this?" If a talk with your physician refutes your evidence, reconsider and back off. If you receive false assurances that you are not dying, then do the following:

2) **State:** "That is not helpful to me. Are you so afraid of my death that you cannot face it?" Even this assertive question will not persuade some to talk about it.

3) Closure: Initiate conversations with individuals about your life together. These include:

Forgiving and letting go of any past pain and differences.

Affectionate reminiscing about past shared events.

Talking about the loved one's future beyond your physical death.

4) Your Needs: What do you want from loved ones? Let this not be a brave, "I will take care of my own needs alone." Make honest requests that meet your needs and enable them to express their love in practical ways. Consider making out a Living Will that limits extraordinary medical steps to maintain your life when there is no longer any hope for living.

5) How do you feel about the dying process? Honestly share your fears, doubts and concerns. Tell about your growth in facing death. Talk about the positive elements of your dying and death.

6) Death and After: Express your own understanding of what occurs at death and after death. Ask others to share their beliefs.

7) Your Funeral: Talk about what you want for your funeral.

8) Affirmations: Express your love to everyone. Say your goodbyes.

9) Prayers: By this time, you know what you want to say and have your own unique way of praying. Take charge of your prayer life and flow in faith with God. Prayers are appropriate as a part of any and all of the above suggested steps. Here is a prayer for the dying process:

A Prayer in the Midst of Dying

God, I know that unless a miracle happens soon, I am going to die.

At times, I am able to accept death. I am tired of the fight for life. I am tired of hurting. In these moments, I accept death, looking to it as a friend. I welcome my transition into a healthy body and a new life in Heaven.

At other times, I feel panic, fear, and anger. I feel trapped in a diseased body. I feel sad that I couldn't find a means for overcoming this disease. I yearn for more time with loved ones and for one more experience of the things that are important to me. I am angered that this is happening to me.

Now prepare for Emotional Release Therapy by placing your dominant hand on your heart and choosing a color symbol for releasing your emotional pain.

Help me to complete any unfinished business. I choose to die in peace. I release my angers, resentments, hurts, disappointments, and fears into my hand, along with any other emotional pain.

Then, with your dominant hand still on your heart, let your hand fill you with God.

God, flow into my heart through my hand. Fill me with your presence, love, joy, and peace. Assure me of your love and of Life Everlasting.

I thank you for the gift of life. I thank you for your presence during my journey. Enable me to look back upon my life with a sense of satisfaction.

It is so strange how my priorities have changed—how the things that seemed so unimportant now have deep meaning.

I place my life in your hands. I know that you are with me in life, in death, and in life beyond death. I trust you. Tend to my needs as I rest in your care. Thank you. Amen.

25

Closing Words

I hope you discovered *Healing Yourself* to be valuable.

If you patiently worked through all the chapters, I am confident that your efforts have dramatically improved the quality of your health, your happiness, and your life.

When I completed *Healing Yourself,* my only regret was that I would not know the joy of personally being with you to share in your rewarding journey back to health.

During the past thirty years, I have helped thousands of people regain their health through wellness counseling and spiritual healing. I estimate that ninety percent of these regained their health. I hope you were able to increase that percentage through your committed efforts and by being equipped with far with better tools for your journey than I initially possessed.

I would like to know about your experiences with *Healing Yourself.*

- What was helpful; what was not?
- How did it improve your quality of your life?
- How did it improve your medical condition?

You can write me at:

Walter Weston
c/o Hampton Roads Publishing Company, Inc.
134 Burgess Lane
Charlottesville, VA 22902

Thanks.

What It Means To Be a Healer

Healing is one of the most joyous and rewarding vocations, but most of us never intended to become healers.

I call my own entry into healing *"God's warped sense of humor."* As a young pastor in 1966, I did not believe in healing. I became a believer one afternoon at a hospital. While I prayed with a dying man, he instantly became well.

Though I now believed, I wanted no part of it. In those days, it could have ruined a United Methodist minister's career. But I discovered that I had no choice. After that initial healing, I discovered that when I held a patient's hand while praying, unintended healing miracles often occurred.

I share this story for your sake. While working through *Healing Yourself,* you may have discovered that you are quite competent in the practice of spiritual healing. By now, you may be fascinated with healing and are becoming obsessed with wanting to know more.

If so, I have the best available resource for you. This is my book, *How Prayer Heals: A Scientific Approach*, of which *Healing Yourself* is a practical companion.

How Prayer Heals offers a complete new scientific understanding of healing. It then proceeds with detailed guidance for doing healing, self-healing, and personal renewal.

26

Support for You and Others

You have been provided all you need to practice self-healing. Everyone who practices it will be richly rewarded.

Two major factors limit you. First of these is not even trying. Reading this book will not improve your health. You must practice its wisdom. Set the date, now, before closing this book.

Decide when you will begin. Set the date and circle it on your calendar. The night before you begin, place positive notes in your bathroom and kitchen that remind you to begin. Without these notes, you will likely never begin. New things are difficult to begin. I wrote this book to help you heal yourself, and not for you to know how you might have healed yourself if only you had gotten started.

The second deterring factor would be quitting after a few days, a few weeks, or a few months. You can learn to practice every exercise described in this book. All new things take time to learn. All holistic practices need time to work. Remind yourself daily,

"I choose to become well. I am fighting for my health (and my life.) My health is my number one

priority. This is the most important thing that I will accomplish today. Daily, I will devote __ minutes to self-healing practices. I am worth it. I choose to become well. I am the only one responsible for my health."

THE SUPPORT OF OTHERS

In addition to loved ones, you may find additional support. If this book was helpful, lend it to a sick friend or buy him or her a copy, so that you can work together. Healing each other then becomes possible. A companion to this book, *Healing Others*, will provide additional resources for doing this.

I may be able to provide you additional support—the names of other people in your area who have read this book. For this to happen, send your name, address and phone number to me. If enough people do this, I can forward their names to you.

Send this information to

Walter Weston
c/o Hampton Roads Publishing Company, Inc.
134 Burgess Lane
Charlottesville, VA 22902

May God bless you on your journey back to wellness.

About the Author

Walter Weston holds a bachelor's degree in psychology from Kent State University and a graduate theological degree from the Vanderbilt Divinity School.

In 1991, he earned a Doctor of Ministry degree in healing research at the International College, Montreal. His faculty advisor was Dr. Bernard Grad, a research biologist at McGill University and the father of healing research with more than 200 healing studies.

Dr. Weston has had the privilege of studying with researchers and healers from a dozen nations. He studied the scientific data, beliefs, theories, practice, and history of healing and prayer in the United States, other cultures, and the world's religions.

While researching healing, he studied and observed spiritual healing as practiced by many churches, as well as learning such techniques as Therapeutic Touch, Reiki, Lawrence LeShan healing, kinesiology, balancing energy fields, Chinese Qigong, spirit healing, and pranic healing.

In 1989, he participated as a healer with Ramesh Singh Chouhan, M.D., in the Chouhan-Weston Clinical Studies at JIPMER regional hospital, Pondicherry, India, that scientifically verified a dozen theories involving the practice of prayer for healing. The videotaping of changing energy fields during the touch-healing prayer encounter provided answers for many troubling questions, creating a helpful new picture.

For thirty years, Dr. Weston served as a United Methodist parish minister. He specialized in counseling, personal growth, and the spiritual journey. He is a veteran of the marriage and family enrichment movement and of holistic health practices.

Walter Weston is presently a professional healer, psychotherapist, hypnotherapist, wellness counselor, and workshop leader. He is the author of *PrayWell: A Holistic Guide To Health and Renewal, Healing Others,* and *How Prayer Heals,* as well as this book.

His most recent work has pioneered Emotional Release Therapy that offers dramatic healing of painful memories and destructive fixated emotional states.

Dr. Weston is president of the Cleveland Association for Holistic Health and a member of the International Society for the Study of Subtle Energies and Energy Medicine.

He lives near Akron, Ohio, with his wife, Dana, a registered nurse. Their great joy is their closeness to their three daughters and seven grandchildren.

Hampton Roads Publishing Company

...for the evolving human spirit

Hampton Roads Publishing Company
publishes books on a variety of subjects
including metaphysics, complementary medicine,
visionary fiction, and other related topics.
For a copy of our latest catalog, call toll-free
(800) 766-8009, or send your name and address to:

Hampton Roads Publishing Company, Inc.
134 Burgess Lane
Charlottesville, VA 22902

e-mail: hrpc@hrpub.com
Web site: www.hrpub.com